SEERS, SHRINES AND SIRENS

SEERS
SHRINES
AND
SIRENS

THE GREEK RELIGIOUS REVOLUTION
IN THE SIXTH CENTURY B.C.

BY

JOHN POLLARD

*Lecturer in Classics at the University
College of North Wales, Bangor*

South Brunswick
New York: A. S. Barnes and Co.

6479
Printed in the United States of America

PREFACE

—◦❧❧◦—

It is hoped that this book may be found useful not only by undergraduates, whether classical specialists or students of Greek civilization and literature, but also by the general reader or Hellenic traveller who wishes to know something about Greek religion. With such readers in view all relevant information has been supplied in the text, while the notes have been kept to a minimum. Key references only are given.

The subject is an age which in Bury's phrase 'witnessed not only a social and political movement among the masses in various parts of Greece, but also an intellectual and spiritual stirring'. The difficulties are notorious, but the fascination of the subject seemed to make the effort worth while, for few would deny that the sixth century B.C. was perhaps the most exciting and important in the history of Greece, which means, in great measure, of the western world. No attempt has been made to deal with all the state cults which flourished between 600 and 500 B.C., even had such a task been possible, but only with the main trends and with what went on at Athens and Delphi where the religious revolution was most marked. At the same time attention has been given to a class of imponderables hitherto ignored in English. Indeed the monstrous Sirens of archaic art have received almost as little notice as the Seers and Sibyls of legend.

My debts to my many distinguished predecessors in the field of Greek religion are manifest on every page. At one time or another I have perused the relevant portions of Farnell's *Cults of the Greek States* and *Greek Hero Cults*, Wilamowitz' *Glaube der Hellenen*, Deubner's *Attische Feste*, Professor Guthrie's *Orpheus and Greek Religion*, Professor Linforth's *The Arts of Orpheus*, Buschor's brilliant but controversial *Die Musen des Jenseits* and Professor Nilsson's monumental *Geschichte der Griechischen Religion*. Among other recent books Professor Dodds' *The Greeks and the Irrational* and editions of the *Bacchae*, works which recalled much salutary advice received while researching at Oxford, Sir Maurice Bowra's *Greek Lyric Poetry*, Professor Page's *Sappho and Alcaeus*, Professor Amandry's *La Mantique Apollinienne à Delphes*, Professors Parke and Wormell's *A History of the Delphic Oracle*, Professor Mylonas' *Eleusis and the Eleusinian Mysteries* and Professor Palmer's *The Interpretation of Mycenaean Greek Texts* have guided me throughout. For the archaeology of Athens I have relied largely on Judeich's *Topographie von Athen*, supplemented by Ida Thallon Hill's admirable handbook *The Ancient City of Athens*, John Travlos' splendid new *Poleodomike exelixis ton Athenon* and Professor R. E. Wycherley's indis-

9

PREFACE

pensable *Testimonia*. I was particularly fortunate in being able to persuade Professor Wycherley to read the proofs, an always arduous and often thankless task, and here record my warm gratitude to him for saving me from more serious error.

I should not like to end without mentioning my teachers. Mr G. V. M. Heap first awakened my interest in the history of the Greek drama more than thirty years ago, while I owe an incalculable debt to the late Mr Jackson Knight for his unfailing encouragement in times of adversity and for setting me on the road. Sir John Beazley and the late Dr Tom Dunbabin taught me almost everything I know about Classical Archaeology, and as junior colleague at St Andrews of the late Professor H. J. Rose I was privileged to draw on the vast treasure-house of learning, irradiated by wit and sanity of judgment, which was unique among contemporary scholars. Even during his last illness he continued to read the first draughts of the chapters of the work which he had inspired and approved, suggesting improvements and indicating faults. To his memory this book is humbly dedicated.

ABBREVIATIONS

—o❧⟫❦o—

AAG	Dinsmoor, *Architecture of Ancient Greece*
A Delt	*Archaiologikon Deltion*
AF	Deubner, *Attische Feste*
AJA	*American Journal of Archaeology*
AJP	*American Journal of Philology*
AM	*Mitteilungen des Deutschen Archäologischen Instituts. Athenische Abteilung*
BCH	*Bulletin de Correspondance Hellénique*
BSA	*Annual of the British School at Athens*
CGS	Farnell, *The Cults of the Greek States*
CQ	*Classical Quarterly*
CR	*Classical Review*
Cf.	See
DF	Pickard-Cambridge, *The Dramatic Festivals at Athens*
DO	Parke and Wormell, *The Delphic Oracle*
DTC	Pickard-Cambridge, *Dithyramb, Tragedy and Comedy*[2]
Eleusis	Mylonas, *Eleusis and the Eleusinian Mysteries*
Exelixis	Travlos, *Poleodomike Exelixis ton Athenon*
GB	Frazer, *The Golden Bough*[3]
Geschichte	Nilsson, *Geschichte der Griechischen Religion*[2]
GRBS	*Greek, Roman and Byzantine Studies*
GHC	Farnell, *Greek Hero Cults*
G&R	*Greece and Rome*
HThR	*Harvard Theological Review*
Ibid.	In the work and passage previously quoted
JDAI	*Jahrbuch des Deutschen Archäologischen Instituts*
JHS	*Journal of Hellenic Studies*
Mantique	Amandry, *La Mantique Apollinienne à Delphes*
Op. cit.	Title of work as already cited
Rhein.Mus.	*Rheinisches Museum für Philologie*
Theatre	Pickard-Cambridge, *The Theatre of Dionysus at Athens*
Topographie	Judeich, *Topographie von Athen*[2]
WOCH	*Wochenschrift für Klassische Philologie*

CONTENTS

INTRODUCTION

Greek history is like a long dark band illuminated by a spot-light. The light falls most brightly on the fifth century B.C. leaving what went before in shadow. Yet the sixth, if less brilliant, possessed all the charm and effervescence of an era of change and immaturity, when vigorous archaic conceptions were still dominant both in literature and art and the eternal elements of Greek belief were being finally moulded into their lasting shape. It was a time when enlightened dictators, known as 'tyrants', flourished and encouraged poets to sing at their courts about love and the beauty which passes. It was the age of prophets like Bacis, of miracle-workers like Aristeas and Epimenides, and sages such as Solon and Chilon. The sixth century again witnessed the spread of mystery cults. The humble agrarian rites of Eleusis attained wide fame, reflecting strange new stirrings of religious conscience in the minds of ordinary men. Indeed religious movements of one kind or another were constantly in evidence throughout the century despite the dawn of rationalism and the growing interest in festivals, including drama, and local cults. This interest was most notable at Athens and merits study as constituting a stable principle amid such disruptive forces as Orphism and Pythagoreanism.

In short the religious revolution of the sixth century B.C. was compound of three main parts: first, and most characteristic, the divinely inspired seers, including the shamans, Sibyl, Pythias, Bacchants and Orphics; second the state cults, including the Mysteries at Eleusis and those of the heroes, whose most tangible symbol was a temple or shrine; third, and most controversial and disturbing of all, the monsters, known variously as Sphinxes and Sirens, of contemporary art.

The importance of this revolution for later religious thought can hardly be denied. The Greek seers contributed much to the prophetic tradition, and Eleusis to Christian mysticism, while the

INTRODUCTION

Sirens, as Weicker and Cumont showed, became the angels of the tomb. Philosophy again owed a great debt to Pythagoras who saw in mathematics the key to the understanding of the world.

CHAPTER I

THE DELPHIC ORACLE

One day in Sardis, capital of ancient Lydia, five and a half centuries before the birth of Christ, king Croesus opened a series of papyrus rolls which his emissaries had just delivered. But as he scanned their contents his look of eager anticipation soon gave way to one of disappointment. It was even as he had feared. The vaunted oracles of the gods had proved themselves false. One only remained unopened, but when he read what it contained he welcomed it with awe. It was the answer returned by the Delphic oracle from far away Phocis in Greece. Though couched in enigmatic verse it was plain to the king that it had guessed his secret and so proved to his satisfaction that it was inspired by truth.

I know the number of the sand, and all the measure of the sea. I understand the dumb, and hear the voice that speaketh not. A savour hath assaulted my senses of a strong-shelled tortoise boiled with lamb's flesh in bronze, both laid beneath and set above.

The meaning of these lines was hidden from all save Croesus, for he alone had devised the ruse which was to decide which oracle's claims were just. Exactly one hundred days after the ambassadors' departure he had busied himself in a highly unkinglike task. First he had dismembered a lamb and a tortoise and boiled them together in a brazen urn. Then the better to keep his action secret he had covered the urn with a bronze lid. The concoction of such an unusual dish would have appeared peculiar even had it been performed by a slave. But when an oriental monarch so far forgot himself as to assume the temporary rôle of chef his behaviour seemed eccentric in the highest degree. It was in effect the very last kind of activity that anyone would have been likely to associate with a king, and that was why Croesus set such store by it. All the oracles claimed to be infallible, but Croesus was prepared to take no risk. It was of vital importance to his ambitions to learn in advance the outcome of an attack which he contemplated launching against his neighbour Persia, whose power was growing every year. Only a genuine oracle could tell him this so Croesus decided to test them all. These, according to Herodotus, were the oracles of Apollo at Branchidae near Miletus, Abae and Delphi in Phocis, of the heroes Amphiaraus and Trophonius in Boeotia, of Zeus at Dodona in Epirus, and of Zeus-Ammon in Libya. The list in itself is a little suspicious in that it is confined, in the main, to the oracular centres famous in the fifth century B.C. One might, for example, have expected Croesus to have first tested the efficacy of shrines nearer home, one of which, that of Apollo at Patara in Lycia, was known to Herodotus, while even those at Grynium in Aeolis and at Claros in Ionia, though their fame belonged to the late classical world, probably existed in archaic times. Herodotus undoubtedly acquired the list at Delphi, where propaganda in the fifth century B.C. concerning events in the sixth was clearly much in evidence.

To these, or at any rate to some of them, the king had despatched his personal ambassadors with strict instructions to inquire of each oracle in turn what he was doing at home in Lydia on the hundredth day after their departure. The extraordinary nature of his activity obviously precluded a happy guess, and when the ambassadors returned with their written answers all but two were wide of the mark. No record survives of the reply received from the Amphiaraion, indeed we are told that Croesus only sent offerings there out of sympathy for the hero, but the Delphic reply was said to have been as already quoted. It pleased Croesus so much that he organized a sacrifice on an unprecedented scale in honour of the Pythian Apollo. All Lydians, as being personally concerned in the favourable outcome of the war, were required to contribute to a holocaust of 300 cattle and innumerable cups of gold and silver as well as couches, robes and jewels. The residue, when melted down, was cast in bricks of gold and despatched to Delphi. There the bricks were raised in a glittering pile with a golden lion to crown them. But this was not all. Indeed there seemed to be no end to Croesus' generosity. Two giant bowls for mixing wine, made respectively of gold and silver, were set up on either side of the temple entrance. Their value may be gauged from Herodotus' description. The historian saw them a hundred years later and stated that the gold one weighed about a quarter of a ton, while the capacity of the silver bowl was more than 5,000 gallons. The king's gifts also included four silver jars, two lustral vases of gold and silver, silver bowls and the golden statue of a woman, known as Croesus' 'pastry-cook', four and a half feet tall. He included in addition a large golden shield which was kept in the shrine of Athena 'Fore-temple'.

It was a staggering offering even by eastern standards, and something quite outside the normal experience of the Greeks. On the strength of it Croesus ordered the emissaries who had delivered the offerings at the Amphiaraion (a shield and a spear of solid gold) and Delphi to pose the burning question: Should Croesus march against Persia? To this was appended the subsidiary inquiry as to whether he should first strengthen his forces with an ally. To these—though Herodotus strangely does not quote the actual words—the Pythia replied that if Croesus marched he would destroy a great empire, and that he must first discover who were the most powerful of the Greeks and make them his friends. Later authorities give the first oracle in the famous version 'After crossing the Halys [a river in Asia Minor] Croesus will destroy a great empire'.

Oracles survive to prove a close relationship between Delphi and Sparta from at least the sixth century B.C. and possibly earlier. The ally mentioned in the oracle was clearly she, and there seems no reason to doubt that the success of Croesus' expansionist policy depended to some extent on the existence of a powerful western alliance. In effect he never mastered Persia, so his pro-Spartan hopes, backed by Delphi, were stillborn. But the king lived as yet in blissful ignorance of the outcome of his ambitions and rewarded the Delphians personally with gifts of money. In return he received the freedom of the city.

He then consulted the oracle a third time, inquiring whether he would reign for long. To this the oracle replied:

Nay, when a mule becometh king of the Medes, flee, soft-soled Lydian, by pebbly Hermus, and stay not, nor feel shame to be a coward.

This reply pleased Croesus too, taking it as he did, at its face value. Obviously a mule would never occupy the Persian throne, so the question of his flight could hardly arise.

Yet when he eventually made war on Cyrus, the Persian king, Croesus' hopes were speedily destroyed. After an indecisive engagement the Persians advanced on his capital Sardis and captured the city after a short siege. Croesus himself was taken prisoner, and sentenced to be burnt on a pyre. It was at that moment yet another oracle was fulfilled. The king had a son, dumb from birth, concerning whom he had approached the oracle. The latter had replied as follows:

Son of Lydia, ruler of men, Croesus, thou prince of fools, desire not to hear in thy halls the voice long prayed for of a son speaking. 'Twould be better for that to be far from thee. He will speak first on a day that is not propitious.

When Sardis fell, the sight of a common soldier advancing on his father moved the youth to cry out in warning:

Wretch, wouldst thou slay Croesus?

The rest of the story is pure myth. When the pyre was well and truly alight and Cyrus had repented too late of his cruelty Croesus prayed to Apollo who sent a rainstorm to quench the flames. Cyrus henceforth treated his enemy with becoming courtesy, and Croesus survived to make an offering of his chains at Delphi. At the same time he despatched emissaries to inquire—and here we begin to sense the fabrication of a Delphic apologia—why Apollo had tricked him. The oracle replied that he had been fated to expiate his ancestor Gyges' crime, and anyhow had not taken the trouble to ascertain to whose empire the god referred, so that on that score at least he had only himself to blame. The defence is, of course, quite illogical, because even if the king had interpreted the oracle aright, his fate was still unavoidable. The story of Gyges was as follows.

According to Herodotus, Candaules, king of Lydia, had a beautiful wife, of whom he was so proud that he discussed her charms with a member of his bodyguard called Gyges. When the latter remained incredulous he invited him to secrete himself in the queen's bed-chamber in order to judge her beauty for himself. But the queen observed him and was so furious with her husband that she incited Gyges to plot his murder. This the guilty pair accomplished and Gyges ruled in his master's stead. The truth of this story probably lies in the second half, and for that Croesus was doomed.

Nevertheless Apollo claimed to have done what he could for Croesus, and had actually deferred his fate for three years. Finally he had saved him on the pyre. As for the reference to the mule, Croesus had been guilty once again of wilful misinterpretation. Had he stayed to investigate the oracle more deeply he might have come to realize that the mule was Cyrus, the child of mixed parents, Persian and Mede. When the answers reached Croesus he accepted them without complaint and admitted that he was solely to blame.

Such is the tale told about Croesus, and as it best typifies the kind of story current in the following century about Delphic activity in the sixth it has been quoted in full. The question is, of course, how much of it could be described as authentic. Herodotus heard it at Delphi where the authorities had clearly been at pains to preserve their reputation by obscuring the details of a flagrant failure in face-saving myth. As the historian gives it the story points an amusing and effective moral. It is, in effect, little more than a bold dramatisation of the familiar Greek dogma, basic at Delphi, that moderation is the best of all practical virtues, and that pride goeth before a fall. Visitors to the restored Alcmaeonid temple of Apollo were suitably appalled by such carved injunctions as NOTHING IN EXCESS, GO BAIL AND DOOM IS NEAR and the best known and highly enigmatic KNOW THYSELF, and it would seem to be a possibility that some at least of these sayings, which were popularly attributed to the Seven Sages, already existed on the archaic temple which was destroyed by fire about 548 B.C. and were transferred to its Alcmaeonid successor of early classical times. 'Nothing in excess' appears first in the sixth century poet Theognis, but the second, which has seemingly a more ancient ring, was said, with the first, by Plato in the Charmides, to have been a later dedication than 'Know thyself'. The myth of Croesus is, in effect, on a par with the stories told about Trophonius and Agamedes, the legendary builders of Apollo's first temple, or of Biton and Cleobis the pious Argive brothers. The former were told by the god to wait seven days for their wages, and were then rewarded with death. The latter once harnessed themselves to a wagon, when the oxen failed to arrive, and hauled their mother, a priestess of Hera, all the way from Argos to the temple across the plain. For this service they were honoured above all other men by their fellow Argives and their statues were set up in Delphi, and have since been located. But the tale told in later times how on the night of their arrival their mother prayed to Hera to grant them both the greatest boon in her power, and how on the following morning they failed to wake, is clearly a moral accretion based on the Trophonius-Agamedes legend. Certainly there is no mention of the deaths of Biton and Cleobis on the inscribed statue bases.

The facts seem to have been these. Croesus sent his gifts in advance in the hope of influencing the oracle in his favour. In this he succeeded. The oracle did all in its power to assist the wealthy monarch, even to the extent of advising him to make a Spartan alliance in Greece. But his ultimate fate it could not hinder. The best it could do was to preserve a series of ingeniously amended post-eventum versions of the oracles which it had sent the king. Doubtless the language difficulty would have raised its own problems, and rendered subsequent amendment easy.

Yet despite the host of wonder stories deliberately fostered to enhance its reputation in later times, Delphi's influence was never higher than during the sixth century B.C.

Delphi was and still is one of the most arresting places in the world. It nestles on a ledge like an eagle's eyrie high up on the bare flank of cloud-capped Parnassus. Behind a bold cirque of precipitous cliffs form a natural amphitheatre. Most impressive of all are the Bright Ones, which seen from afar reflect the summer sun like beacons of fire. Below, the horizon drops away into the echoing nothingness of the Pleistus gorge. The only sounds are the cool plash of the Castalian spring issuing from its black spout, and the sullen roar of the distant torrent tumbling down towards the Gulf. High above the endlessly wheeling vultures and eagles lend an air of doom to the scene not unremarked by augurs. For nowhere else in Greece are the great raptorial birds, whose predatory habits provided augurs with ready omens, so plentiful as at Delphi. Aeschylus describes the neighbouring Corycian cliff as 'bird-haunted', while a recent writer in Country Life described how he watched a lammergeyer, grandest and rarest of all the vultures, gliding across the canyon. Apollo's own connection with augury is referred to in the Homeric Hymn to Hermes, which may date from the early sixth century B.C.

> whoever shall come
> In answer to the cries and flight of birds of sure omen,
> He shall have joy of my voice, and I will not deceive him.
> But whoever puts his trust in birds that chatter idly
> And seeks to inquire of my prophetic powers against my will,
> And to apprehend more than the immortal gods,
> I say his journey shall be fruitless.

From this Professor Amandry deduced that it was the science of ornithoscopia, i.e. to say prediction by observing the flight and cries of birds, that was practised at Delphi, rather than ornithomanteia or divination.

Some evidence too for a concern with birds is provided by the story, preserved by the historian Philochorus, that a certain Boeo prophesied at Delphi and was the authoress of a work entitled *The Generation of Birds*.

Yet, though the background remained doubtless pretty well the same, Delphi in 600 B.C. must not only have presented a very different appearance from that familiar to us today, but also from that with which Plutarch, who held priestly office there during the first century A.D. was acquainted, or Pausanias, the guidebook writer, who flourished during the second. On a levelled space, west of the exit of the Castalian spring, stood the old temple of Apollo, which was destined to be destroyed in a fire half a century later. Of the details of its construction or appearance we know virtually nothing as a few fragments of limestone and terracotta roof-tiles are all that survive. Probably it was a less pretentious version of its renowned successor, which was rebuilt through the efforts of the exiled Alcmaeonids, formerly members of Athens' most powerful clan. Whatever its actual details it was regarded as a masterpiece by the author of the relevant portion of the Homeric Hymn to the Pythian Apollo, and housed Croesus' treasures.

The temple stood virtually alone. Of stadium, theatre, club, and round-chamber, and all the noble treasuries soon to be dedicated by the various city-states, there was, as yet, no sign. A notable exception was the treasury of Cypselus, tyrant of Corinth,

to which Croesus' offerings, together with those of his predecessors, were removed after the fire. The first Pythian games
was still to be celebrated, though some form of musical festival
was probably held. At any rate Pausanias preserved a tradition
that Orpheus, the fabled lyre-player, had disdained to compete
in the Delphic contest of song. Again the bare space, sacred to
Earth and Themis, as has been proved by the discovery of statue
bases dating from the fifth century B.C., may have marked the
spot where the pre-Apolline oracle, despite Professor Nilsson's
scepticism, was believed to have had its beginning, hard by the
gaunt rock pulpit where the wandering eastern seer, known as
Sibylla or the Sibyl, was said to have prophesied. The tradition
that the Sibyl visited Delphi is only found in late authorities, but
I have elsewhere advanced reasons in favour of the hypothesis that
the story could have arisen in archaic times. The only other
buildings of note, apart from the Pythia's house and the Delphians' homes, were the archaic temple of Athena, surnamed
Foretemple, which occupied a site below the Apolline shrine, the
precincts of heroes like Phylacus and Autonous, which, according
to Herodotus, stood respectively by Athena's temple, and by the
Castalian spring, and possibly the prototypes of the tombs of
Pyrrhus and Dionysus which were shown there in later times.
There may also have been shrines of Apollo's mother and sister,
Leto and Artemis, who are mentioned in an inscription quoted by
Demosthenes' rival Aeschines.

Yet, despite the comparative dearth of buildings and the
absence of public games, the oracle's fame was already established, and pilgrims came flocking to Crisa or Cirrha, which is first
mentioned in Homer, and appears, to judge from the Hymn to
Apollo, to have given its name to the entire district. Its importance traditionally depended upon its highly strategic position
across the most frequented route to Delphi, and whether it
levied dues or not it managed to excite the jealousy of the
Amphictyonic Council. These 'dwellers round about' consisted
in the main of Thessalian and Dorian tribes, who were centred
on Anthela, a little-known shrine of the corn-goddess Demeter
situated in the neighbourhood of Thermopylae. But they held a
watching brief for all the shrines in the neighbourhood, of which
Delphi was the chief. Such, at any rate, seems to be the most
likely explanation for the subsequent war which so effectively

destroyed Crisa's power that in time even its site was forgotten. Recently, Mr W. G. Forrest has proposed that the war was fought not on its behalf, but for the possession of Delphi which was acting in the interests of Crisa. The authorities are late, and it is clear that by classical times the details of this war had been either forgotten or had become confused with those of later sacred wars.

The period following the first Sacred war—traditionally dated in 594 B.C.—was perhaps the most important in Delphic history. The oracle's fame outshone that of her many rivals in Greece and Asia, and in the end all but a few faded into insignificance. Henceforth Delphi became the political and spiritual arbiter of the entire Greek world.

Broadly speaking the political history of Delphi is not difficult to assess. Its religious history is more obscure. Why Delphi rather than other more accessible shrines should have become the most important cult centre in Greece has given rise to much speculation. In Anatolia the oracles of Apollo at Patara and Branchidae were presumably well known even in archaic times, and the god also divined at Corope in Thessaly, at Abae in Phocis, at Tegyra, Ptoon and Thebes in Boeotia, and at other places like Claros and Grynium of admittedly more dubious antiquity. Boeotia also boasted an oracular shrine of the hero Amphiaraus, as well as the seat of Trophonius. Yet Delphi's supremacy was already recognized from an early age. Pytho's 'rocky threshold' was known to Homer, and despite Nilsson's warning that the passages in which it occurs may belong to the latest strata, the cumulative Mycenaean evidence is impressive. To deny the importance of the idols found beneath the temple foundations on the grounds that they possibly formed part of a fill leaves Mycenaean Pytho without a serious *raison d'être*. If no oracle was in being in pre-Apolline times, despite Aeschylus' statement in the *Eumenides* that it had formerly belonged to Earth and Themis, it is difficult to account for the existence on the site of Mycenaean remains. The presence of the idols, one of which appears to be seated, Pythia-fashion, on a tripod, has to be explained. Indeed even if they originated lower down the hillside in the vicinity of the Marmaria then, as Fontenrose has recently suggested, the shrine of Athena Foretemple could still mark the original oracle of Earth.

Fortunately we are not here concerned with Delphic pre-history, though enough has been said to suggest that the most probable reason for the oracle's fame was that it dated from Myceanaean times. It is with the brilliant Apolline usurpation that the story of classical Delphi begins, though both the date and the manner of the god's advent are equally obscure. Whether Apollo was in origin the Babylonian Aplu as Professor L. R. Palmer has recently suggested or not, the particular form of his cult which first reached Delphi appears to have been that of the Dolphin from Crete. Such at any rate was the view of Cynaethus, the author of the Homeric Hymn to the Pythian Apollo, who doubtless reflected Delphic dogma at the close of the sixth century B.C.

The coming of Apollo's cult seems to have coincided with the beginnings of Greek colonization, and this cannot but be significant, as Corinth, Delphi's most influential neighbour, was a leading colonizing power. Her early alliances are quite uncertain, but if, as has been recently suggested by Mr Forrest, they included Chalcis and Thessaly, the political value of an oracle situated close to the Gulf is sufficiently obvious.

Yet despite the speciousness of the political argument it is hard to resist the conclusion that there were deeper reasons too. An oracle does not acquire world fame purely on political grounds. It must be eminently successful in divining the future, or, what amounts to the same thing, men must believe in its success. Yet men will not believe in an oracle's truth unless it at least preserves the illusion of infallibility, even when occasionally open to bribery as it certainly was. That the Delphic oracle did in effect succeed in preserving its reputation for infallibility from the time of Croesus and throughout the testing period of the Persian Wars is a remarkable fact of history. How it did so is hard to assess in detail, though technique accounts for much.

The methods of divination practised at other Apolline oracles were far less well organized than that adopted, or perhaps one should say with greater probability, inherited at Delphi. At Branchidae the vehicle of inspiration was water, and the priest interpreted as he chose. At Ptoon, some form of possession seems to have been practised as the prophet gabbled in an unintelligible way. The will of the Ismenian Apollo was interpreted by the inspection of burnt offerings, and that of the Spodian, also at Thebes, by listening to the voices of birds. At Patara the priestess prophesied from omens, or by gazing into water, and to help her foster inspiration, was incarcerated for a time in the temple. At Argos she drank the blood of a lamb, sacrificed at night, in order to achieve a like end. At least so much we glean from Pausanias.

It seems safe to assume that by 600 B.C. the ancient Pythian ritual, whether directly adopted or modified by the Apolline, had achieved its permanent form. Of its details we know nothing during the sixth century B.C. though something may be surmised. In a century when prophets and seers were prominent the fame of the Pythia ranked high. There is indeed a remoteness and dignity about the earlier oracle which contrasts sharply with the intimate glimpses of Roman Delphi offered by Plutarch. Yet for all the aura of awe and mystery with which the Delphians found it profitable to surround their shrine, nothing was obviously left to chance when emissaries of the wealth and importance of Croesus arrived upon the scene. The stage-managing, we may take it, was less elaborate than that described by Plutarch, though presumably in essentials much the same.

How frequently the oracle functioned in archaic times is unknown, though according to Plutarch it was only once a year. Certainly it appears to have worked overtime during the Persian Wars, and previously séances may have been less frequent. The practice of employing a *proxenos* or sponsor to intercede with the Delphians on the inquirer's behalf is mentioned by Euripides in the Ion, and so was presumably old. Thus extraordinary séances could presumably have been arranged when circumstances demanded, always provided that the god was in residence at the time. But even during the period of his three months' absence among the Hyperboreans, the mythical people who inhabited a fairyland in the far north, a lot-oracle probably answered the questions of casual visitors, and such as were unable to afford the cost of a full Pythian séance. Our knowledge of this oracle is slight. According to a copy of a convention dating from the fourth century B.C. the choice between two alternatives was decided by drawing one of a pair of beans. For its existence in earlier times we have Plutarch's tale about Aleuas the Red, who became king of Thessaly when the Pythia drew his name inscribed on a bean.

The archaic fountain of the Castalian spring has now been discovered, but whether it was there or in the spring called Cassotis, mentioned by Pausanias, that, before dawn on the seventh of the month, the Pythia underwent ritual purification, prior to being escorted by the priests to the temple, archaeological investigation has not finally determined. Diodorus of Sicily, the Greek historian of Roman times, says the Pythias were originally maidens, but that one forgot her vows, so that later married women were preferred. Nevertheless they were expected to wear maiden costume, live apart from their husbands in a special house, and practise ritual chastity. In fact the emphasis on chastity appears to have been purely titular, and the result of a practical compromise. It probably reflected the change of function which the Pythia underwent when she ceased to be the priestess of Earth. The fruitful earth mother, or her Mycenaean equivalent, might have been expected to be hostile to celibacy even in a priestess. Apollo, on the other hand, had always demanded celibacy in those he favoured, as the legends of Cassandra and the Sibyl show. Neither might marry, though Cassandra was said to have been raped by the lesser Ajax, and subsequently enslaved, and once the god had endowed them with the gift of true prophecy he was powerless to take it away.

Not only the Pythia herself, but the priests, known as *Hosioi*, also suffered lustration, as indeed did those who wished to consult her. From Pindar downwards the texts refer to clients 'descending' into the place of consultation, yet there is no archaeological support for anything in the nature of an underground chamber within the shrine. Possibly something of this nature formerly existed at Delphi, and long after consultants ceased to descend into the Pythia's presence the inherited ritual verb remained. Possibly again, as Fontenrose has suggested, there was in prehistoric times some religious association with the Corycian cave, which is mentioned by Aeschylus, and lies some miles to the north of Delphi. However this may be the most that the archaeological evidence will allow is that there was probably an inner room beyond the outer vestibule, screened off in some way and set at a slightly lower level.

In this inner room stood the *omphalos*, the sacred navel, which was said to mark the centre of the earth, or, by some, the site of the tomb of the monstrous Python, which Apollo slew when he first came to Delphi.

Before the Pythia was admitted to the shrine a goat was led

in by the priests and sprinkled with holy water to see how it would react. If it shivered properly it was sacrificed and the séance was allowed to go forward. Arrived in the sanctuary the Pythia mounted the tripod, itself an extraordinary and unique procedure whose significance has been much discussed. Probably little credence can be given to the comic poet Aristophanes' vulgar suggestion in the Plutus that the Pythia conceived the spirit of Apollo while so seated, though Doro Levi has produced evidence from ancient Crete to show that the tripod set over a fire for the purposes of sorcery came to be regarded as a symbol of mantic power. Next she prophesied, according to the Homeric Hymn, 'from the bay', whatever the precise significance of the phrase. Whether she actually chewed the plant, in order to induce some form of stupefaction, always assuming that the bay can stupefy, as Sophocles implies in a fragment from a lost play which contained the advice 'After eating bay be careful to bite your lip', i.e. to say keep your secrets to yourself, or whether she merely functioned in close association with the god's sacred tree are questions which we cannot answer. Possibly the custom varied with the centuries. Later the plant was apparently burnt in order to give off incense, if that is what Aristophanes meant in the Plutus by 'shaking the bay'. Squatting on the tripod the Pythia awaited the moment of divine inspiration in a mood which doubtless varied with the temperament of each. Plutarch records how one unfortunate woman, when forced to prophesy against her will, suddenly went mad. Her frenzied behaviour put the priests to flight, and so overwhelming was her distraction that she died. That few Pythias were so powerfully moved seems probable, but that the majority regarded themselves as divinely inspired there seems no reason to doubt. Even now it is hard to be at Delphi and remain a sceptic, and in the days of Croesus few men were.

As for the actual details of consultation, they probably did not differ in essentials between the archaic period and later times. After offering a ritual cake, the cost of which served in place of a fee, the inquirer was required to sacrifice sheep or goats on the holy hearth in the presence of the sponsors and priests, who claimed a portion of the victims including the skins. Only then was the inquirer admitted to the vestibule and warned to remain silent and think pure thoughts. Inquiries might be verbal or submitted in written form to the officiating priest who was styled the

Prophet. He in turn dictated the Pythia's reply either orally or rendered, presumably with assistance, into hexameter or more rarely iambic verse. According to Pausanias a tradition existed at Delphi that a Hyperborean called Olen had invented the hexameter, but neither the date nor the circumstances of its introduction are known. It was at this stage that forgery or manipulation became possible, as the inquirer was not in the presence of the Pythia, and was consequently debarred from interpreting for himself.

The dating of oracles is notoriously hazardous, and particularly when they are mentioned by later authorities in connection with events popularly associated with an indeterminate past. Notorious among such was the cruel penance levied by Apollo on the Locrians of Opus when they begged for his help in the alleviation of a plague. They were informed by the oracle that Athena was still angry for the outrage on Cassandra perpetrated by Ajax in her temple at Troy, and that this was the reason for the plague. In order to be rid of it they were ordered to continue to despatch two maidens to the Troad until such times as the wrath of the goddess was appeased. The authorities for this barbarous story do not admittedly antedate the fourth century B.C. but the terms of the oracle appear so harsh that scholars have been unwilling to refer it to a contemporary era. If Demetrius of Scepsis, the antiquarian of the Troad, had good grounds for connecting the oracle with the period of Persian suzerainty then it could be referable to the sixth century B.C. Even then it may simply have represented a revival of something far older and grimmer. However that may be two maidens were duly abandoned on the Troad's inhospitable shore with instructions to make their way to Athena's temple. If the local inhabitants saw them the penalty was death. When they reached the temple they lived out their lives in harrowing poverty keeping the building clean. The story sounds incredible, but serves to highlight a sinister side of Greek religion which is not always apparent. Nowadays, if a plague strikes a country or city, men turn to science to aid them in their difficulties. If hospital accommodation is inadequate the authorities may build more, while research establishments are set up to investigate the nature of the disease. But in ancient times it was believed that only the bringer of plagues could take them away. Apollo, like most deities, was ambivalent. He could visit men with a plague whether of mice or death, as he did in Homer, and, if appeased, could remove it. Plagues were a serious matter. Only by propitiating the deity could men be freed from them. When hundreds died the lives of two mere girls was a small price to pay for the relief of suffering, and as Delphi was the accepted arbiter in all such matters, her findings, based on harsh but logical interpretations of mythology, were accepted without question. All Greeks believed in the Ajax story. Athena had been offended, and had to be appeased. Delphi, who had become, since the seventh century B.C., the chief means of obtaining freedom from the taint of blood-guilt, was now the curer of plagues. She alone had Apollo's ear, or at least a greater share of it than other shrines, so that when she told the Locrians what they must do, they carried out their penance without question, and continued to do so into late classical times.

Athens too suffered from a plague at the beginning of the sixth century B.C. According to one tradition Solon, who in a century devoted to miracle workers was himself regarded as semi-divine, sent Epimenides, the Cretan wizard, to Delphi to bring back advice. Whatever the truth about Epimenides, whose dates are as vague as his historical reality, there is reason to believe that Athens had links with Delphi at least from the beginning of the sixth century B.C. Solon is said to have sent an Athenian contingent to fight with the Amphictyons during the first Sacred War, and also to have appointed two official representatives, known as *Exegetai Pythochrestoi*, to act as intermediaries between the oracle and the city. The choice of the individual representatives was said to have been left to the Pythia, who selected them from a list of ten. The archons again were placed under oath by Solon, and the penalty for breaking it was the dedication of a life-sized statue of gold at Delphi. All this we may not believe in detail, but it is a pointer to Athenian aspirations to be friendly with the chief shrine in Greece.

Though not proof against the wealth of the Lydian kings the Delphi of tradition displayed consistent hostility towards the Greek tyrants. But it is hard to sift the genuine from the false, and many of the so-called oracles are little more than moral maxims coined after the event. Typical of such is the story about Polycrates, most famed, perhaps, of all the tyrants. He had refounded the festival on the neighbouring island of Delos, where Apollo was said to have been born. He then approached Delphi with a view to learning whether she would like the festival to go by the ancient name of 'Delian' or whether she would prefer it to be called 'Pythian'. The oracle is said to have replied laconically: 'Whether Delian or Pythian it's all the same to you.' Soon after Polycrates, at whose enlightened court in lovely Samos all the leading poets gathered, was captured by a Persian satrap and put to death on a cross.

A typical case of pollution occurred at Ephesus in the middle of the century when the tyrant Pythagoras slew his opponents, who had taken refuge in a temple. When a plague and famine followed the frightened tyrant inquired of Delphi what he should do. The oracle replied that he must build a temple in the place of the one which he had polluted, and pay due rites to the dead.

An involuntary act of pollution occurred when the army of Alyattes, Croesus' predecessor, had the bad luck to destroy a temple of Athena which stood near a field of burning corn. When the king fell ill he approached the Pythia, but she declined to reply until the temple had been restored. Alyattes in his anxiety to curry favour built two temples instead of one, and honoured Delphi with an enormous silver mixing bowl on a welded iron base which survived right down to the second century A.D. when Pausanias saw it. Herodotus states that it impressed him even more than the offerings of Croesus and the other eastern kings. Doubtless this gift, like those of Croesus, was sent in advance in the hope of influencing the oracle in Alyattes' favour. But the wonder still is that an oriental monarch honoured Delphi at all.

A grisly story of pollution was told about the inhabitants of Phocaea in Asia Minor, who went out to colonize Corsica in the sixth century B.C. They were driven from the island by the Carthaginians, and some of the prisoners fell into the hands of the Caeretans in southern Italy and were stoned to death. Later the spot where this atrocity was committed was haunted and people passing it became distorted or paralysed. On Delphi's advice the Caeretans sacrificed to the murdered Phocaeans, and the haunting ceased.

Delphi's rise to fame during the archaic period was closely connected, as has already been observed, with colonization. It was a novel and dangerous matter to leave one's country and to

seek fresh homes abroad, and religious sanction for such enter-
prises were sought and given by the chief oracular seat. But most
of the oracles which refer to events in the sixth century are
clearly *post-eventum* propagandist efforts. Typical of these was the
oracle supposed to have been given by the Pythia to the Dolonci
of the Thracian Chersonese, who were seeking settlers to aid
them against their enemies. They were told to choose the man
who first offered them hospitality in Greece. This turned out to
be the Athenian Miltiades, who did in fact found a settlement in
the peninsula in question.

That the Pythia was open to bribery Herodotus bears witness.
Nevertheless the offerings of the Lydian kings did not meet with
the success for which they could have hoped, though that was
probably not Delphi's fault. The Alcmaeonids, the powerful and
brilliant Athenian family who were back in exile after opposing
the tyranny of the Pisistratids, were obviously not swayed entirely by religious motives when they undertook the rebuilding
of Apollo's temple after the disastrous fire. The propaganda value
of the restoration was sufficient to unseat the Athenian tyrants
when Sparta intervened against them at Delphi's instigation. So
high indeed was the oracle's reputation at this period that
Cleisthenes, the political reformer, is said to have requested the
Pythia to choose the names of the ten new tribes.

Some few oracles bear the mark of genuine age. Notable among
these is the Pythian response to the Siphnians. The inhabitants of
this tiny island had, during the sixth century B.C., through their
flourishing gold and silver mines, become rich beyond their
dreams. Alarmed lest their good fortune should excite the envy
of the gods they sent to Delphi to inquire whether it was
destined to continue.

The oracle replied as follows:

> But whenever in Siphnos the city hall becometh white, the market-
> place white-browed, then the wise men ought to beware of an ambush of
> wood and a herald all red.

The references to 'white' and 'white-browed' were to the
gilding of the buildings in question with precious metals. Then
a few days later the island was visited by Samian pirates sailing
in ships with red prows. They captured some of the inhabitants

and held them to ransom for a sum of a hundred talents. This, as Parke and Wormell point out, was hardly a sum to cripple the city, and suggest that the Delphic answer represented a near accurate forecast of the kind of disaster which was likely to befall a small wealthy state. In effect a sudden inundation by the sea put an end to the mines of Siphnos, and this natural cataclysm the Pythia failed to foresee. Yet second-sight, if the Pythia possessed it, and there is reason to suppose that some Pythias did, tends to refer to immediate events and not to long-term disasters. This is the kind of oracle that makes even the sceptic wonder whether, whatever the degree of manipulation by the priests involved, the pronouncements of the Pythia herself were not seldom genuine.

Delphic honesty was not all it might have been if we can believe the legend about Aesop, the famous teller of fables. According to tradition he was a slave by birth, and sent as an agent by Croesus to Delphi. But his biting attacks on their beggar-like way of life made him unpopular with the Delphians, and they engineered his ruin by causing a gold cup, destined as an offering, to be found among his personal effects. The story is clearly apocryphal, but illustrates the manner in which the priests were regarded as dealing with their enemies.

The story of how a fisherman called Demarmenus once drew up a shoulder-bone in his net is typical of the kind of problem with which the oracle was expected to deal. Here, as so often, mythology was of assistance. Pelops, as everyone knew, had been served up as a dish to the gods by his father Tantalus in order to prove whether the former could distinguish between human and animal flesh. Fortunately the subterfuge was discovered, but not before Demeter had bitten a piece out of the victim's shoulder. Hence when the gods brought the hero to life again the missing part was replaced with ivory. The fisherman's bone was in Delphi's view the piece which Demeter had spat away. Again the oracle had been lately visited by an embassy from Elis when the event occurred, and it was with Elis and Olympia that Pelops was particularly associated. As the embassy was seeking a cure for a plague the solution was naturally obvious. Pelops' missing shoulder must be restored to the land where the hero had first earned fame by tricking Oenomaus and marrying Hippodamia. So the blade was sent back and jealously preserved as a precious relic at Elis.

The curious story about Aristeas who, like Oedipus and Amphiaraus, did not die in the normal fashion, but disappeared from the earth, and then went one better than the Theban heroes by turning up alive and well two and a half centuries later in southern Italy, was typical of the tales told about miracle workers during the sixth century B.C. Aristeas' date is naturally quite uncertain, but when the men of Metapontum consulted the oracle after his second disappearance it expressed agreement with the magician's own explanation that he had followed Apollo in the form of a crow. Underlying the tale, which seems to possess Pythagorean features, was, it seems, an historical Aristeas who wrote a poem on the Arimaspi, the legendary people who hoarded gold. Possibly during the sixth century some impostor with the same name attempted to impress the credulous by claiming to be the poet. Delphi then solved the problem in the most effective way open to her, which obviously did not include casting doubt on the wizard's authenticity.

The oracle which gave official sanction to the practical ethic of moderation was, not unnaturally, linked in legend with the Seven Sages. The names, which varied, included a statesman like Solon, Thales the first philosopher, Periander, tyrant of Corinth, as well as less famous characters concerning whom little or nothing is known. The oracles in which they figure, though based on popular stories, reflect the Delphic attitude to mortal presumption in the sixth century B.C. The man who inquired who was wiser than himself was liable to receive a salutary snub. When Chilon, the Spartan sage, and Anacharsis, the traveller, posed the question they were told that an obscure Myson of Oeta was wiser than either of them. Again when a wealthy Magnesian offered a huge sacrifice in honour of the god, and then inquired who was the most pious of men, he was informed, to his consternation, that a certain peasant was who had offered only a handful of barley. A similar story was told about Gyges of Lydia, who expected to be called the happiest of mortals. Instead the oracle named a poor husbandman working on the monarch's plot. Of course neither Chilon, Anacharsis or Gyges ever posed such questions in fact, nor if they had would the priests have so insulted them by replying in this vein. Nevertheless this was the kind of answer doubtless with which Delphi was associated, and represented just the kind of moral that she tried to drive home.

The possibility that the frenzied type of possession associated with the devotees of the god Dionysus may have influenced the Pythia has been hotly debated. Wherever the new religion arrived it maddened the women and sent them howling over the mountains like banshees, waving their cone-tipped wands. Everywhere the new force appeared irresistible, but with the passage of time the worship of Dionysus became part of the state canon with a resultant civilizing of its rites. At Delphi too the god was welcomed, though it is hard to deduce at precisely what period. He was certainly associated with the region of the Corycian cave in Aeschylus' time, and later, if we are prepared to accept their authenticity, oracles were pronounced advising doubters to accept the god's worship. Anyone again, according to Philochorus, the fourth century B.C. historian, could see Dionysus' tomb in the sanctuary at Delphi in his own day, but he tells us nothing of the date of its establishment there. Parke and Wormell have suggested that as the plan of Apollo's temple did not vary in essentials from the sixth century B.C. it might have proved impracticable to have introduced a tomb into the sanctuary after the destruction by fire of the archaic temple in 548 B.C. But Herodotus states quite clearly that the Alcmaeonids, 'since they were very wealthy and members of an old and famous family, proceeded to build the (new) temple on a far more magnificent scale than the plan demanded'. Hence Dionysus' intrusion into the sanctuary could have occurred at the time of the rebuilding in 510 B.C. However that may be it would have been easy for the Delphians to have attributed any existing or anonymous monument they wished to Dionysus whenever official recognition of his worship was considered politic. Professor Fontenrose refuses to believe that any monuments could have become so neglected that their original dedication was forgotten, but the Delphians would scarcely have scrupled to alter or modify any tradition to suit their purpose, and Greek mythology, as Fontenrose himself has so ably demonstrated in *Python*, was accommodating to a degree. Cynaethus' failure to mention Dionysus in his interpolated edition of the Homeric Hymn, and the like silence of the early sixth century lyric poet Alcaeus, could be explained on the grounds that it might well have been considered impious to introduce mention of another diety's worship in a hymn or ode composed in honour of one specific god. But the date of the Alcmaeonid temple might explain this difficulty too. The Delphians had doubtless been long aware of the growing influence of the Dionysiac religion in neighbouring Boeotia, and became steadily more anxious to gain credit for spreading it elsewhere in Greece. Dionysus, further-more, was a minor god of prophecy and operated an oracle in Thrace as well as at neighbouring Amphikleia. These factors coupled with the growth of Orphism must have weighed heavily in the final decision to admit Dionysus, in the capacity of junior partner, to the headquarters of the Apolline religion. So the legend that he had died there, or that he relieved Apollo during the latter's three months' sojourn among the Hyperboreans, was fostered, and oracles supporting the Dionysiac religion became, during the fifth century B.C., increasingly common. The Thyiads again, whose torch-light ritual among the steeps of Parnassus is movingly described by Sophocles in the Antigone, as well as by Euripides in the Ion and Aristophanes in the Clouds, were brought under the control of the Delphic *Hosioi*, and the Orphic worship of Dionysos Liknites, the child deity of the winnowing fan, may also have been introduced at the end of the sixth century B.C.

Professor Palmer's recent reminder that it could be argued, in view of the occurrence of Dionysus' name in two Mycenaean Linear B texts, that his worship preceded that of Apollo at Delphi, is weakened, as he himself admits, by the possible occurrence of Apollo's own name in a text in the form *Diwos huius*—Son of Zeus, but also by the lack of an old literary tradition.

Yet despite the official recognition of a highly alien faith Apollo still reigned supreme at Delphi during the sixth century B.C., the deified embodiment of an attitude of mind. This was, of course, the characteristic Greek sense of sober reverence for the powers which irrationally govern the earth. Yet they were only irrational from the point of view of men whose mortal limits prevented them from divining the meaning behind. Only through the medium of Loxias, the Slantwise Interpreter, could they be ad-mitted to the counsels of Zeus. 'The god of Delphi neither re-vealeth, nor concealeth, but hinteth,' as Heraclitus said. It was left to each recipient, even though he were as great and powerful as Croesus, to interpret the oracle for himself.

For all the efforts of modern scholarship there is an element about Delphi which defies research. It is somehow symbolized by the mysterious wooden E, the meaning of which sorely puzzled Plutarch, and remains unexplained today.

NOTES TO CHAPTER I

Page 17. Croesus. Cf. Herodotus, 1, 6 ff. and 26 ff.

19. Sparta. Cf. *DO*, 1, pp. 82 ff. and 133 ff.

20. Candaules. Cf. Herodotus, 1, 7 ff.

21. Delphic Inscriptions. Cf. *DO*, 1, pp. 386 ff.

    Cleobis and Biton. Herodotus, 1, 14 and 15. Cf. Tod, *Greek Historical Inscriptions*, 3.

22. Raptorial Birds. Cf. Pollard, 'The Lammergeyer', *G&R*, January 1947; 'Birds in Aeschylus', *G&R*, October 1948.

    Boeo. Cf. Pollard, *AJP*, LXIX, 4, 1948, p. 358.

    Augury. Cf. Amandry, *Mantique*, p. 57.

23. Temples and Alcmaeonids. Cf. *DO*, 1, pp. 143 ff.

24. Oracle of Earth. Cf. Nilsson, 'Das delphische Orakel in der neuesten Literatur', *Historia*, 7, 1958, p. 239.

    Sibyl. Cf. Pollard, 'Delphica', *BSA*, 55, 1960, pp. 195 ff.

    Phylacus and Autonous. Cf. Fontenrose, *The Cult and Myth of Pyrrhos at Delphi*, pp. 199 ff.

    Leto and Artemis. Cf. Aeschines v. Ctes, 107.

    Crisa. Cf. Forrest, 'The First Sacred War', *BCH*, 80, 1956, pp. 33 ff.

25. Oracles of Apollo. Cf. Nilsson, *Geschichte*[2], 1, p. 545 and refs.

    Fontenrose, op. cit., p. 254.

26. Aplu. Cf. *Proc. Class. Assoc.*, 1963, p. 32.

    First H. Lewy, *Woch.*, 1893.

    Forrest, 'Colonization and the Rise of Delphi', *Historia*, 1957, pp. 171 ff.

27. Lot-oracle. Cf. Amandry, op. cit., pp. 33 ff.

    Archaic fountain. Cf. Orlandos, *BCH*, LXXXIV, 1960, pp. 151 ff.

    Cassotis. Cf. Amandry, op. cit., pp. 138–9; Pouilloux et Roux, *Énigmes à Delphes*, 1963.

28. Pythia. Cf. *DO*, 1, p. 35; Holland, *AJA*, XXXVII, 1933, p. 211.

    Cassandra. Cf. Mason, *JHS*, 1959, pp. 80 ff.

    For discovery of false omphalos cf. Nilsson, *Historia*, 7, 1958, p. 239.

29. Tripod. Cf. Doro Levi, *AJA*, XLIX, 1945, No. 3, p. 305.

    Bay. Cf. Amandry, op. cit., pp. 129 ff.; *DO*, 1, p. 26.

    Skins. Cf. Daux, *Hesperia*, XVIII, 1949, pp. 58 ff.

30. Demetrius of Scepcis. Cf. Leaf, *Strabo in the Troad*, p. 193.

32. Phocaea. Cf. Herodotus, I, 167.

33. Dolonci. Cf. Herodotus, VI, 34.

    Bribery. Cf. Herodotus, V, 63; VI, 66.

    Cleisthenes. Cf. Hignett, *A History of the Athenian Constitution*, p. 131.

    Siphnians. Cf. Herodotus, III, 57; *DO*, I, p. 151, p. 163, note 23.

34. Aesop. Cf. Herodotus, II, 134; Wiechers, *Aesop in Delphi*, 1961.

    Demarmenus. Cf. Pausanias, V, 13, 5; Parke, *Hermathena*, XXIII, pp. 153 ff.

35. Aristeas. Cf. Herodotus, IV, 15, 1; Dodds, *The Greeks and the Irrational*, p. 141; Bolton, *Aristeas of Proconnesus*, 1962.

36. Corycian cave. Cf. Aeschylus, Eumenides, 24 f.

    Temple. Cf. Herodotus, V, 62, 2 f.; Parke and Wormell, *DO*, I, p. 11; Fontenrose, op. cit., p. 194.

    Cynaethus. Cf. Wade-Gery in *Greek Poetry and Life*, pp. 56 ff.

    Alcaeus. Cf. Page, *Sappho and Alcaeus*, pp. 244 f.

37. Thrace. Cf. Herodotus, VII, 111.

    Amphikleia. Cf. Pausanias, X, 33, 10.

    Hyperboreans. Cf. Plutarch, *De E ap. Delph.*, 389 C.

    Thyiads. Cf. Sophocles, *Antigone*, 1126 f.; Euripides, *Ion*, 1125 f.; Aristophanes, *Clouds*, 603.

    Dionysos Liknites. Cf. Farnell, CGS, V, pp. 167 and 188.

    Mycenaean evidence. Cf. Palmer, loc. cit., 32–3.

    For a recent attempt to distinguish between the Greek and un-Greek attitudes to oracles and seers cf. H. Klees, *Die Eigenart des griechischen Glaubens an Orakel und Seher*, 1965.

CHAPTER II

THE CULTS OF ATHENS

A rumour that their patron goddess had been observed driving through Attica in her war chariot had been current in Athens for several days. Then, as more and more people claimed to have seen her, the excitement became intense. When she finally entered the city and a herald proclaimed that the goddess had come in person to welcome back her favourite, the exiled Pisistratus, the entire population fell down in worship. In fact it was not the goddess at all, but a local giantess called Phya who had been persuaded to don armour and ride through the streets. Such is the story told by Herodotus, who ridicules the ease with which the Athenians, 'who were generally regarded as surpassing all other Greeks in intelligence', were taken in. Assuming, as seems certain, that the story is apocryphal, it is still of interest as exemplifying the ends to which the tyrant was believed to be prepared to go in order to persuade the citizens that their own patron deity was anxious for his return. Clearly it was to Pisistratus' advantage that his name should be linked with that of Athena as closely as possible, and whether he achieved his aim by crude pageantry or some other means we shall probably never know. It is again significant that it is the goddess's martial aspect which is uppermost in the legend, a side which had been mainly in abeyance throughout the archaic era and only re-emerged when the tyrant came to power. Doubtless the average Athenian citizen had always visualized Athena Polias as roughly identical with Homer's war goddess, just as the other members of the pantheon probably tended to be seen through the Bard's eyes. It was, nevertheless, as the promoter of the city's welfare in all its aspects, including even marriage and the rearing of children, and as the patroness of both men's and women's crafts that Athena was worshipped in early Athens. She was also, in her capacity as state protectress, naturally concerned with the fertility of the crops, and in particular of the olive, upon which the community depended for its food and trade. At the same time and despite all her universal qualities the position of Athena in the archaic period, vis-à-vis the old local deities and heroes of the Acropolis, was curiously at variance with her later fame. Indeed in some ways it appears to have been rather that of a privileged equal than of a supreme deity who controlled the city's destiny.

At the beginning of the sixth century, to judge from the archaeological evidence, or rather the absence of it, Athena lacked even a temple of her own. This omission was not remedied until many years later when the Pisistratids built the Old Temple mentioned in the inscriptions, or surrounded with a peristyle a Solonian edifice raised some time before. Even then it was her remarkable association with the Attic hero Erechtheus which was remembered in legend and cult alike.

In the Iliad it is stated that the goddess 'reared' and then 'established' Erechtheus 'in her own rich temple', while in the Odyssey she is said to enter his 'goodly house'. Moreover offerings of bulls and rams were made to the hero by the youth of Athens at annual festivals, though there is no mention of like honours being paid to the goddess. The Greeks themselves were puzzled by this curious alliance and to explain it propounded the following myth.

Hephaestus, god of volcanic fires and, by analogy, of workers in metal, wished to marry the maiden goddess whose marked aversion to anything suggestive of sex was partly explained by her extraordinary birth. According to an ancient story Athena had no mother but sprang fully armed from the head of Zeus. Hephaestus himself assisted at the accouchement, splitting the god's skull with a shrewd blow from an axe. Ever after the goddess remained a virgin and when Hephaestus assailed her she defended herself with her spear. In the end her amorous suitor failed to rape her and discharged his seed upon the ground. Earth thus fertilized gave birth to Erichthonius or Erechtheus—the two are usually distinguished in legend—who assumed snake form or anguiform extremities. This was a symbolic way of indicating that he was, as we should say, a genuine 'son of the soil'—in fact autochthonous —home-born and bred as all Athenians proudly claimed to be, and being earth-born like the serpents, who lived in holes in the ground, a promoter of fertility in the soil from which he sprang.

Earth handed the snake-child over to Athena, who put him into a chest. This she entrusted to the daughters of Cecrops, king of Athens, to watch over. They were strictly charged not to open the chest, but mastered by curiosity like Pandora or Eve, two of them, Aglauros and Herse, peeped inside. So terrified were they by the monster within that they leaped from the Acropolis to their doom. Only Pandrosos remained faithful to her trust and her sanctuary on the citadel still survives.

The facts which lie behind the legend seem to be something like this. A thousand years before the days of her classical fame Athens was ruled by Mycenaean kings, whose splendid tombs, or those of their nobles, have been found in the flanks of the rocky hillock, known as the Areopagus, where the most venerable Council met. They dwelt in a palace whose foundations have been uncovered on the north side of the Acropolis adjacent to or partially covering the sites of all the oldest sanctuaries. Since Athena, as Nilsson showed, and the inclusion of her name in a Linear B tablet proves, was in origin a Mycenaean goddess who protected and prospered the fortunes of the house, then the old tradition that she formerly lived not in a separate temple, but in the palace with the king, died hard at Athens. The king, like the coeval Egyptian pharaohs, was doubtless regarded as a sacral being whose sanctity extended to the palace where he and the powerful house goddess dwelt. The latter crowned, as was usual in Mycenaean times, a high and impregnable citadel, which itself through its association with the palace and the king was regarded as in some sense holy. Hence it is hardly surprising to find that the area on its summit next to or actually standing on the site of the ancient palace was generally regarded as the most sacred in the city.

It included in addition to the old shrine of Erechtheus, which was destroyed, according to Herodotus, in the Persian sack of 480 B.C., the tomb of Cecrops, reverently bridged over in the later Erechtheum, the precinct of Pandrosos, the altars of Zeus *Hypatos*—Highest—perhaps because a bolt had struck the Acropolis at that point—Hephaestus, and the mysterious hero Butes, whose name means 'Neatherd'. Farnell suggested that he was the mythical ancestor of an agricultural clan, the *Butadae*—literally 'Sons of the Neatherd', who worshipped Erechtheus. There too were shown the marks of Poseidon's trident and the well of salt water where waves could be heard. Close by in Pandrosos' sanctuary grew the sacred olive which Athena had planted when she and the sea-god were rivals for the land. The gods, or Cecrops himself, according to legend, had awarded the goddess the verdict preferring the humble olive to the promise of glory at sea. The Athenians too, according to Herodotus, kept a snake on the Acropolis which was regarded as its guardian, and possibly as an epiphany of Erechtheus the autochthonous king. When it was finally decided towards the end of the fifth century to honour all these cults in a conjoint shrine, the intimate association between the ancient Mycenaean monarch and the old palace goddess was perpetuated by the provision of adjacent chambers in the new temple of Poseidon-Erechtheus. By then Erechtheus had long been identified with the sea and earthquake god. How this came about we do not know, though Farnell's suggestion that the title Poseidon-Erechtheus represented a primitive alliance between an Ionian community which worshipped Poseidon and an ancient Attic folk which revered Erechtheus, the hero-king who promoted fertility, is an interesting possibility.

That Athena was worshipped alongside of, and not as essentially superior to, Poseidon and Erechtheus, Cecrops, and other old Acropolis heroes and heroines at the beginning of the sixth century B.C. appears, in the light of the building of the Erechtheum to preserve all these cults, at least a reasonable inference. Then came the success of Solon against Salamis and the nationalist spirit which may have been reflected in the building of an original Parthenon, if in fact such a temple ever existed, began to come to the fore. Probably only then did the worship of the eponymous goddess begin to outshine that of other cults. Finally Pisistratus came to power, and his advent witnessed a still more dramatic change.

The tyrant and his sons absorbed themselves in religious matters, partly doubtless for political reasons and partly to increase national prestige. They founded new or elaborated existing temples on a scale of magnificence hitherto unknown in mainland Greece. The new temple of Athena Polias, i.e. the 'Old Temple' of the records, was surrounded with a magnificent peristyle of thirty-two columns. It was further embellished with splendid pediments representing the battle of the gods and the giants. Possibly too there was a frieze representing, as in the later

Parthenon, the Panathenaea, which steadily gained importance during the sixth century B.C., and to which games were added in 566 B.C.

This festival dated traditionally back to the days of Theseus. It was celebrated on Athena's birthday, the 28th of *Hekatombaion*—'the month of the sacrifice of a hundred head of cattle'—which owing to the vagaries of the ancient calendar cannot be fixed more precisely than some time in July or August, and every fourth year, that of the Great Panathenaea, with special splendour. Later the Pisistratids added Homeric recitations, and provided a stadium for the Panathenaic games. These like the Olympian and the other Greek athletic festivals were religious in character and not, as today, purely secular events. The competitors strove for fame and glory, and the victors were presented with jars of olive-oil bearing figures of the goddess.

Even prior to the Pisistratid elaborations the procession of the citizens to the Acropolis during the Great Panathenaea must have been a moving and impressive event. The purpose of the procession was to honour the goddess by supplying her with a new robe. The origin of the custom may have been the very practical one, as H. J. Rose has suggested, that the ancient wooden image got cold in winter and naturally needed clothes. The robe itself was woven for the goddess by the women of Athens assisted by two *arrephoroi*. The latter were two young maidens selected to bear the 'unutterable objects' in the festival of that name. The robe was a considerable work of art embroidered with battle scenes like the Bayeux tapestry, only in this instance the subjects were taken from mythological wars.

The concourse proceeded from the Kerameikos, a district which included far more than the local cemetery, to the Eleusionion, the temple of Demeter and Kore. It returned to the Acropolis where a solemn sacrifice of cows was held at the altar standing before the temple. After the sacrifice the cows' flesh was distributed among the worshippers, as was the usual custom when the deity was not an underworld power. Heading the procession were the *kanephoroi*—the basket-bearers, maidens of high birth and irreproachable character, with both parents living and so untainted by death, who were privileged to carry the baskets or vessels of gold and silver which contained the first-fruits, sacrificial knife and garlands. They were magnificently dressed, carried parasoles, and wore jewellery as well as strings of dried figs. No modern May queen ever excited the extraordinary jealousy that the election of these girls incurred. Indeed the assassination of Hipparchus, Pisistratus' younger son, by the later famed tyannicides Harmodius and Aristogeiton, was said to have been provoked by the gratuitous insult laid by the tyrant on Harmodius' sister, a *kanephoros* in the procession, when her brother declined to become his lover.

In the fifth century the robe was spread on a ship's mast erected on a ceremonial car, and so carried to the temple. This strange custom could have arisen after the rise of Athenian sea power, or been borrowed from the Great Dionysia. The robe could have been displayed in some simpler way during the sixth century B.C. Behind the basket-bearers came the beasts for sacrifice, followed by the citizens, mounted and on foot, with the old men carrying olive branches in the goddess' honour. On this occasion too men were permitted to bear arms, which gave the tyrannicides the opportunity they were seeking. There were also mock fights, while boys danced in armour. Yet the most impressive single feature of the entire festival was the Torch Race which took place on the evening preceding the procession. It consisted of a kind of relay race between companies of runners, with a lighted torch in lieu of a baton.

Athena not only received a new robe at the great Panathenaea, but also a robe washing at the Plynteria, the festival of the bath. The details of this festival we learn from Xenophon and Plutarch. Athena's temple was covered up, a custom which some interpreted as boding ill, and no Athenian would undertake any serious business on that day. Though no account survives from archaic times it seems unlikely that the details of such a comparatively simple ceremony changed much, if at all, in the interim.

Two 'laundresses' escorted the wooden cult image down to the sea at Phalerum, which was Athens' original harbour before the development of the Piraeus. The procession was attended and directed by an Athenian family, the Praxiergidae, who claimed the privilege by ancestral right. Upon arrival at Phalerum the statue was unwrapped, its robes washed, and then the procession returned again by torch-light to Athens. Its mood, we are told, was mournful as the ceremony was supposed to have been founded in memory of Aglauros, Cecrop's daughter, after whose tragic death the women were said to have left their clothes un-washed for a year. During the same month, and possibly in associ-ation with the Plynteria, some form of Spring-Cleaning festival was held in honour of Athena. Probably it included a ritual brushing out of her temple, but no details have survived.

The ancient wooden statue of the goddess, which, according to tradition, had dropped from heaven, was presumably kept in the Old Temple prior to its destruction by the Persians in 480 B.C. Nothing is known concerning the ritual or customs associated with this temple apart from the interesting veto which prevented Dorians from entering the precincts. The occasion of this veto has not been explained, though there is evidence that Athens was successful in resisting the Dorian invasion—namely the last wave of Greek invaders into the pre-Hellenic world, which over-whelmed the country about 1000 B.C.

One of the most exciting archaeological discoveries ever made was the finding of the marble *korai* or maidens. Most of these charming statuettes, with their demure archaic smiles, old-fashioned robe styling and delicate Ionian-type workmanship, were found lying in a pit on the Acropolis near the N.W. corner of the Erechtheum where they had been buried as part of the débris after the Persian sack. Others lay scattered abroad in the rubble with traces of the original paint-work still fresh upon them. Their purpose and provenance is disputed. The custom of dedicating statues or similar offerings to deities was widespread, and characteristic of the archaic era in Greece, as is known from the large number discovered in temple ruins. Some considered that the statues were intended to represent her worshippers or even the goddess herself. But the discovery of an inscription recording the offering of a maiden by a fisherman to Poseidon, suggests that they were merely standard offerings and intended to represent no one in particular. The proximity of the pit, where the majority of the statuettes were found, to the site of the Old Temple, together with their late sixth century style, is strong evidence that they were dedicated there. Certainly there could have been no more charming way of honouring the goddess in her new home than by arranging with a sculptor to provide a statuette in keeping with the worshipper's taste and means.

In general the indications are that in the Old Temple Athena's martial aspect was restricted to the mythological battles portrayed on the pediments in which she was a notable contestant. The Older Parthenon, which appears, like its great Periclean successor, to have been designed to impress foreigners with the city's growing might, was pre-Persian and never completed. The ancient poros, i.e. tufa stone sculptures which were found buried on the Acropolis, are too archaic in style to have belonged to the Old Temple and have been assigned by experts to an early Parthenon, founded about 570 B.C., which is thought to have occupied the same site as its two successors. Whatever the truth of the matter the difference between the Parthenon and the Old Temple seems basically to have been one of *mood*. The Old Temple was founded to enhance the fame of the Pisistratids, the Parthenon to foster the nationalist spirit.

As the bringer of victory Athena was worshipped in a separate shrine. During the latest reconstruction of the famous fifth century temple, which commands the prominent bastion east of the Acropolis gates, the foundations of its predecessor were discovered together with an altar, inscribed in letters of the mid-sixth century B.C. This temple, like the others, was destroyed by the Persians together with the ancient wooden image whose home it was. As this image was 'wingless' and classical Nikai or Victories were represented in art as graceful winged maidens, the temple retained its unusual nickname right down into modern times.

With regard to the altar base it is important to realize that temples were not regarded primarily by the Greeks as places of worship, like Christian churches, but rather as the homes of deities where they could be visited and honoured with dedications. The more serious business of sacrifice took place at the altar outside. Again the officiating priests were not professional holders of the office, but ordinary Athenian citizens on whom the privilege had fallen either by right of birth, because certain priesthoods were a family concern, or by virtue of state office. In fact the secular and religious sides of life which tend to be divorced in northern European countries were rarely distinguished in ancient Greece.

Athena's dual aspect as a great goddess of state, and at the same time as the popular deity who watched over the humble tasks of the people, is well exemplified by her title Ergane—Patroness of Toil. In this capacity she possessed a sacred enclosure east of the entrance to the Acropolis, at least from Pisistratean times. Her festival was the Chalkeia—the Smith Feast—which was held during the month of Pyanepsion, at roughly the same time as Bonfire Night. Hephaestus was naturally concerned in the ritual, but Athena had the chief part. Sophocles refers to the festival in a memorable fragment, and the details would not have changed significantly in the intervening years.

> On your way all ye folk of handicraft
> That honour the grim-eyed Worker, Zeus' girl,
> With winnowing-fan set upright.

From this it is deduced that winnowing fans were set up along the route followed by the procession, but that is all we know.

Athena was also worshipped in the same vicinity under the cult title of Hygieia—goddess of Health at least as early as the sixth century. As such she appears to have ante-dated the conception of Hygieia as an independent goddess. She was also surnamed Apatouria after the clan festival of that name, and it was the custom of her priestess to call upon newly wedded couples bearing the aegis—a magic goat-skin decorated with a Gorgon's head—which was Athena's special emblem. It seems curious to hear of the virgin goddess in this connection, but as State Protectress the welfare of the family was very much her concern. As Clan Protectress Athena was worshipped in the Agora—the civic centre—under the cult title of Phratria, and also possessed a shrine as Boulaia—She of the Council.

Athena also represented the power of law as is clear from the legend about Orestes. When Agamemnon returned from Troy his wife Clytaemnestra, aided and abetted by her paramour Aegisthus, murdered him in his bath. Her daughter Electra and son Orestes determined to avenge their father, and the latter slew the murderers. Now guilty of matricide the unfortunate youth was pursued by the Erinyes or Furies, the living embodiment of the victim's curse. He was finally tried by the ancient Athenian court of the Areopagus and acquitted by Athena's casting vote.

In ancient Greece the murder of a private individual was regarded as a purely personal affair. On the other hand the murderer was treated as being under a curse and liable to exile for pollution. It was an important duty of the Areopagite Council to examine suppliants and, if they considered their cause a righteous one, to absolve them from this taint. In a chasm beneath the Areopagus, the Erinyes were worshipped under the title of 'Kindly Ones', or *Semnai*, 'Revered Ones'. Both, judging from their titles, may have been originally benevolent earth spirits with whom the grim Erinyes were hopefully identified. The name Areopagus suggests a connection with Ares, the hated god of war, who was remembered in myth if not in cult. According to Euripides Ares had a daughter by Aglauros, who was ravished by Halirrhothios—the Sea-roarer, son of Poseidon. The latter was slain by the angry god, who appeared as a suppliant at the first meeting of the Council and was there acquitted of homicide. Throughout the sixth century the Council of the Areopagus acted as the guardian of the constitution, and its political power did not decline until the middle of the following century.

The strangest ritual of all held in honour of Athena was connected with the *Arrephoroi*, the maiden bearers of the 'unutterable objects'—for that is what the title seems to mean—who assisted in the preparation of Athena's new robe. Two duty girls, who according to the women in Aristophanes' comedy *The Lysistrata*, were often as young as seven years old, lived in a house on the Acropolis not far from the Old Temple. Who guarded or looked after them at such a tender age we are not told, though it seems safe to assume that they were generally kept under the wing of the priestess of Athena. On the day of the festival, which fell during Skirophorion—equivalent to our June—they carried out by night the following curious rite. The priestess gave them certain secret objects whose identity was likewise unknown both to herself and to them. These they placed on their heads and bore to the precinct of Aphrodite in the Gardens by a subterranean walk. There they left their burdens and returned with others in their place. Their task completed the *Arrephoroi* were relieved of their duties, and two other little girls took their place. So much we learn from Pausanias, who implies that the details were not generally known in his day.

An important scholium or note on a passage in the late dialogue writer Lucian offers the suggestion that the 'unutterable objects' were pieces of dough modelled to resemble 'serpents or male

shapes'. The latter were presumably phallic, though much uncertainty attaches to the scholium in question, as festivals and
rites are confused almost past redemption. Snakes would certainly
suggest a fertility cult. Again the objects were taken to the sanctuary of Aphrodite, who was connected with fertility and sexual
desire. In Athens there seem to have been two sanctuaries of
Aphrodite in the Gardens, one on the southern flank of the
Acropolis and the other, which has only recently been discovered, on the northern. The latter, which was sacred also to
Eros, god of love, contained several altars, while stone representations of the male sexual organ were found scattered about.
Broneer, the discoverer of the sanctuary, suggested that as no
burnt or blood offerings were permitted to stain the altars of
Aphrodite in Paphos, the phalloi themselves were the objects or
at least the occasion of veneration, probably to increase the fertility of the seed-corn. What may be an actual representation of
the ritual act will be described in the following chapter.

The Arrephoria then shows that Athena's rôle as State Protectress included in its wide purview the promotion of fertility. But
whether it had always done so is a matter for serious doubt. An
inscription states that a certain Nausistrata 'ministered both to
Athena Polias and to Pandrosos while she was serving as an arre-
phoros'. Now Pandrosos means 'All Dew', and dew is a valuable
commodity in Attica's parched land. She therefore was in origin
a nature deity, and not a king's daughter, whose functions were
later usurped by the more powerful Athena. The inclusion of her
sanctuary in the later Erechtheum, and the planting of the sacred
olive there, is then explained.

Again the youths of Athens took their oaths of loyalty at the
shrine of Aglauros on the precipitous north wall of the Acropolis
over which, frightened by Erichthonius, she had once incontin-
ently leaped. Aglauros too appears to have been an agricultural
deity in origin, for her name means 'Bright One', an epithet of
the dew, who like her sister became associated with an important state cult. In fact the trio—for Herse also means 'dew'—
were regarded as powers of sufficient importance to be honoured
with cults on the Acropolis alongside the goddess of state.

Athena's connection with agriculture was further commemorated in the festival of the Procharisteria or Thanksgiving, held at
the beginning of spring when the corn was beginning to swell. Its

importance may be gauged from the presence of the magistrates who sacrificed to the goddess in the hope of a good harvest later in the year.

So much history reveals about Athena, but to assume that she was merely a strongly personalized embodiment of contemporary religious conceptions is to forget that her worshippers did not create her but inherited her from the distant past. Indeed it might not be entirely fanciful to claim that she herself was largely instrumental in making the Athenians what they were.

Zeus, the sky and weather god, like his daughter Athena, possessed no notable temple at Athens until the Pisistratids built the Olympieion. At least two shrines and altars raised in his honour graced the archaic Agora, while he possessed three altars on the Acropolis and was worshipped under the title of 'Agoraios', the deity who presided over popular assemblies, both in the civic centre itself and on the Pnyx or Parliament Hill. According to Thucydides the oldest part of Athens outside the Acropolis lay in the area 'towards the south' bounded by the river Ilissus. There stood, and still partly stands, the great temple of Olympian Zeus, 'the Cloud Gatherer', who was imagined, appropriately enough, as dwelling on the highest summit in the land. There too were the temple of the Pythian Apollo and the precinct of Dionysus in the Marshes. The site which the Pisistratids chose for their temple was, according to local Athenian tradition, the spot which witnessed the final receding of Deucalion's—the Greek Noah's—flood. It was also claimed that he had built a temple there. Whatever the truth about a predecessor the Olympieion was consciously designed to surpass in grandeur, and consequently in fame, all other mainland temples. Unfortunately the Pisistratid dynasty did not survive long enough to carry through a project which Aristotle compared, not unjustly, to the building of the Egyptian pyramids, and six hundred years were destined to pass before the temple was finally completed by the emperor Hadrian in ornate Roman Corinthian style. But for all its glory its conception was political and not religious like the early Acropolis shrines.

Zeus was a sky or weather god, and it was this aspect rather than the Homeric conception of an aristocratic paterfamilias that prevailed at Athens in the pre-Pisistratid era. Yet the proximity of the altars of Zeus Hypatos—'Highest' or 'Uppermost'—and of Zeus Herkeios, 'Fore-court', like his more familiar title of 'Xenios', 'Welcomer of Guests', to the site of the former Mycenaean palace suggest that his ruling-class associations were dimly remembered though doubtless in a wider and more popular form. Of the rites practised at these altars we know that no flesh or wine might be offered at that of Zeus Hypatos, but only cakes. The sanctuary of Zeus Polieus, 'Protector of the State', the male counterpart of Athena, stood on the highest point of the Acropolis north-east of the Parthenon. In this capacity the god was honoured with an important annual festival, the Dipoleia, the details of which, like so many others, have been preserved for us by Pausanias. It fell at full-moon during the last month of Skirophorion—June. The most arresting feature was the Bouphonia or Ox-slaying, a ritual unprecedented in Greek religion. Some grain was offered on the altar of Zeus, and an ox was permitted to approach and eat it. In so doing it was, of course, technically guilty of sacrilege and was at once slain by the bouphonos, or 'ox-slayer', with an axe. After slaying the ox the bouphonos dropped the axe and fled. By a curious aberration of Attic law inanimate objects could, if they were agents of killing, be put on trial. In this case, the axe, the instrument, and not the slayer, was held guilty of murder and solemnly cast into the sea. In other words the axe was turned into a scapegoat, and in this way the slayer escaped the danger of pollution from contact with a sacral beast. For since the ox had already eaten the corn from the altar it was presumably regarded as in some real sense holy. So much seems clear, but the general meaning underlying the ritual still baffles analysis.

The Pandia, literally the festival of 'All Zeus', is something of a mystery. There was a hero-shrine on the Acropolis of king Pandion, who was said to have succeeded the snake-king Erichthonius or to have been Erechtheus' grandson. He was supposed to have first introduced the worship of Dionysus, god of ecstasy, to Athens, and the Pandia followed the Great or City Dionysia. But Zeus is derived from the root di, meaning 'bright-sky', and the possibility that Pandion may have been created out of the name cannot be disregarded.

In his civic capacity as Boulaios—Counsellor—Zeus possessed a shrine in the Agora alongside that of Athena. The foundations of the archaic Bouleuterion—Council-chamber—have been discovered, and there must have been kept the god's old wooden image which is mentioned by Pausanias. Zeus was also, like his daughter, concerned with the welfare of the old Attic clans, and was worshipped under the title of Phratrios—Clan Protector— in the civic centre.

Zeus, the sky-god, possessed, illogically, chthonian—i.e. underworld counterparts. One of his titles was Meilichios, 'Gracious One', and his festival, the Diasia, was one of the most important in the Attic calendar. It fell during the 'flower' month, Anthesteria—our February—and was held, according to Thucydides, 'outside the city'. At this celebration the citizens indulged in a kind of spring Christmas when guests were welcome—a characteristic Zeus feature—and children were given gifts. The sacrifice took place at night, as was usual with underworld powers, and the god was offered swine or cakes shaped in beast form, all of which were burned. At a normal sacrifice to upper-air deities where real beasts were slain only certain portions of the flesh were offered to the gods, the remainder being distributed among the priests and the citizens at large. But when sacrifice was made to a chthonian power everything was consumed. In the case of Zeus Meilichios the burning of the cakes was regarded as a symbolic way of indicating that the city was now rid of its accumulated guilt. The god was regarded as existing in snake form because, like Erichthonius, he was connected with the earth. Once he had been propitiated the citizens felt that he would remain 'gracious' towards them for the remainder of the year.

In addition to his function as a ridder of pollution Zeus enjoyed legal powers analogous to those of Athena. Pollution included homicide, and he was worshipped under the cult titles of Hikesios, god of Suppliants, and Phyxios, god of Appeal, probably from very early times.

The Maimakteria, celebrated in November, in honour of Zeus Maimaktes, an ancient cult-title explained by the lexicographers as meaning 'troublesome', was obviously designed to propitiate the deity who controlled the autumn storms, and as such became associated with the god of the weather. The year closed at mid-summer with the Diisoteria, a festival held appropriately enough in honour of Zeus and his daughter Athena in their joint capacity as 'Saviours of the State'.

It should be admitted at once that most of the details which have come down to us concerning the festivals mentioned above are preserved in post-classical authorities, But most of them are so simple and primitive that even when more material evidence is lacking, such as the old wooden statue of Zeus in the Athenian Council chamber mentioned by Pausanias, it is clear that the majority descend from very ancient times. Thucydides mentions the Diasia in connection with the conspiracy of Cylon, an Olympian champion of 640 B.C. who aimed at the tyranny and was advised by the Delphic oracle to try his luck while the citizens were busy celebrating 'the grand festival of Zeus'. This the champion assumed referred to the Olympic Games, which were held in the god's honour, when the Pythia, as open to misinterpretation as ever, had referred to the Athenian Diasia. The result of the attempt was inevitably failure, and the would-be tyrant narrowly escaped with his life.

Hesiod, who flourished probably at the end of the eighth century B.C., tells an obscene story about Zeus' father Kronos. Earth, his mother, grew so weary of Uranus', i.e. of Heaven's, embrace that she encouraged her son to castrate his father. This Kronos accomplished with a blow from a sickle, and Earth was relieved of Heaven's pressure by the Titans coming between. Finally Kronos married his sister Rhea and ruled in Uranus' stead. Learning that he was fated to be overthrown by one of his children he swallowed them all in turn. But Zeus, the youngest, was saved by Rhea, who deceived her cannibal spouse with a stone wrapped in swaddling clothes. Zeus then dethroned his father and reigned as chief god in his place.

Kronos was worshipped at the festival named after him at Athens, on the twelfth of Hekatombaion in July or August, as well as at Olympia, where his hill, the Kroneion, is a prominent feature. It was a harvest festival of a merry nature when masters entertained their slaves. Whatever Kronos' real origin, and in the light of Hesiod it is hardly surprising to learn that he was identified with Moloch and associated with child sacrifice in Rhodes, both the Athenians and Thebans regarded him as primarily an agricultural deity. As far as they were concerned Kronos belonged to an older generation of indigenous gods formerly worshipped in Greece.

The close association between Athens and Delphi which developed during the sixth century B.C. has been mentioned in the previous chapter. The temple of the Pythian Apollo stood in the oldest part of the city outside the Acropolis, and, nearby, the altar, dedicated by the tyrant's grandson, Pisistratus the Younger, has been discovered. There was also a second sanctuary of Apollo Pythius on the north slope of the Acropolis. Strabo refers to this sanctuary in connection with the Pythais, a sacred pilgrimage to Delphi whose purpose was to bring back holy fire. The signal for the commencement of the expedition was a flash of lightning from Mount Parnes, the highest summit in Attica. The ritual was known to Euripides, who mentions it in the Ion, for it was in a cave on the north slope of the Acropolis that Apollo was said to have ravished Creusa, Erechtheus' daughter and Ion's mother. There has been considerable controversy concerning the relationship between the two shrines as well as the probable site of the hearth of Zeus Astrapaios —Bringer of Lightning—from which the flash was observed. What seems reasonably certain is that there was an ancient shrine of Apollo, perhaps under the cult title of Hypakraios—'Near the Summit'—on the north face of the Acropolis in archaic times, and that it was associated with the pilgrimage which may have started in the sixth century B.C.

Of more local interest to all Athenians was the tribal deity Apollo Patroos, the Ancestor, a title also conferred on Zeus. The division into four Ionian tribes, traditionally borrowed from Miletus, took place in prehistoric times. Every citizen was a member either of the Aigikoreis, the Argadeis, the Geleontes or the Hopletes, names possibly once connected with tribal gods. But in the course of time the old deities were forgotten, and all claimed common descent from Apollo Patroos whose shrine stood in the Agora. Apollo, after all, was the father of Ion, the eponymous ancestor of all Ionians, and the Athenian tribes had Ionian names. The phratries again or clans into which the tribes were subdivided also worshipped Apollo Patroos and Zeus Herkeios—the friendly Forecourt deity.

The difficult question of what a title like Apollo Patroos or Zeus Herkeios meant to the ordinary Athenian during the sixth century B.C. or indeed at any other era is complicated almost past solution. Clearly the generalized conception of a deity in all his functions was something from which the Greek mind recoiled. If the Greeks thought of Apollo at all it would have been as Homer described him. But within the sphere of the state religion they preferred to worship the gods in their localized and functional aspects. This, of course, was only natural. If a man desired help on a question affecting his family it seemed more natural to approach Apollo in his specific function as an ancestor god, rather than as the remote Far-darter of Homer. If he wished to approach the greatest god of all on a question of state, his appeal was likely to be more effective if offered at the altar of Zeus Polieus, whose specific business it was to attend to such matters, rather than if made direct to the weather god.

The chief festival of Apollo was called the Thargelia which was named after the penultimate month, May, and was shared by his sister Artemis. It was notable for an event every bit as primitive and strange as the ox-slaying at the Dipoleia. Apollo was a ridder as well as a bringer of plagues, and the opportunity was taken, as at the Diasia, of ridding the city of its accumulated evil by off-loading it, as it were by ritual means upon two human scape-goats or pharmakoi. The latter, both men, were chosen for their hideous appearance and after being adorned with dried figs, black for the men and white for the women, they were driven out of the city and forbidden to return. That the rite was an old one is testified by Aristophanes who says in the Frogs that contemporary politicians wouldn't even have qualified to be scapegoats in the good old days. The Thargelia was concluded with the cooking and offering of the first fruits of the harvest to Apollo. At first it seems odd to find the god of prophecy connected with agriculture. But one of Apollo's titles was Nomios—Herdsman—the deity who prospered the flocks. When the people who worshipped him turned to tillage the transference of his favour from pastures to crops was both natural and easy.

At the Pyanepsia or 'Bean-boiling' held in October on the seventh of the month, Apollo's sacred day, the god was solemnly presented with a dish of pulse porridge, doubtless to win his blessing on the bean and allied harvests. On the same day bands of children appeared in the streets carrying the eiresione or 'wool-pole'. The latter consisted of a branch of bay or olive wreathed with wool and hung with fruit, cakes, bread and miniature jars of wine, oil and honey, which they collected from the houses as they passed along. Finally the wool-poles were hung on all the doors as a token of good luck. Aristophanes has an amusing refer-ence to the custom in his comedy The Knights.

'What's all this noise?' Demos thunders. *'Get away from my door. You've torn my wool-pole to shreds——'*

Originally the custom may have had nothing to do with Apollo, but in time it became a feature of both the Thargelia and the Pyanepsia. As Apollo was a powerful deity it was of signal importance to gain his favour. So one of the boys was chosen to hang up a wool-pole in his temple. The boy selected had, like the kanephoroi in the Panathenaea, to have both parents living as the risk could not be taken of contaminating a holy rite with death, which was regarded in ancient times as a physical thing.

A lesser festival connected with Apollo was the Metageitnia held during August, the month of 'Change of Neighbours', with obvious social implications. The Boedromia, which fell in September, was held to honour the god's war-cry. In the Persians of Aeschylus the Athenians are said to have raised the 'Paian'—Apollo's sacred cry—before attacking the enemy fleet at Salamis, while Aristophanes refers to a festival under this name. But too little is known about the details of such minor feasts for it to be profitable to include them here.

A curious survival from primitive times, and allied to the practice of setting up 'herms', was the erection of pillars in honour of Apollo Aguieus—god of Highways—outside street doors. Aguieus is a good example of what Usener described as a 'Sondergott', i.e. a functional deity not yet fully personalized. Probably the pillars had nothing originally to do with Apollo, unlike the 'herms' which had a clear connection with Hermes. Their purpose was doubtless to ward off evil from the houses outside which they were erected, including plagues, which were Apollo's special province, and in his honour they were wreathed with garlands.

Artemis, Apollo's sister, embodied many of the attributes of a primitive nature goddess. Her character was bivalent like that of her brother, for she was not only a patroness of hunting, but the protectress in particular of females in young. There was no close season for hunting in ancient times, but there did exist a powerful religious tabu against killing in the breeding season, which men flouted at their peril. At Brauron in Attica little girls played bears in her honour. A recently discovered series of vases, some of which date from the sixth century B.C., depict them naked, or wearing short kirtles. They also dance with lighted torches or wreaths before an altar or palm. Possibly, as Madame Kahil has suggested, they are mourning for Iphigeneia, as Brauron was in the neighbourhood of her tomb. A goat, the typical rustic offering, was sacrificed to the goddess, and the entire ritual, known as the Brauronia, was repeated annually at Athens. It was a women's festival and presumably ancient as it is referred to by Herodotus. That the Mistress of Beasts should have been associated with bears, the largest and most formidable carnivore in Greece, or have been regarded on occasion as an embodiment of a bear herself, is not surprising. But apart from one vague reference to a similar 'fawn' ritual at Larissa, the picturesque details of the Brauronia are unique. One of Artemis' traditional titles was Kalliste—Fairest—a circumstance which may have contributed to the Arcadian myth about the maiden Callisto. She, like so many other fair women, suffered the misfortune of being loved by Zeus. Hera, out of jealousy, transformed Callisto into a she-bear, who, according to one tradition, was shot by Artemis. So the bear association existed at least in myth, but it is curious to find it at Athens. Probably it was due to the importance of Brauron in archaic times, which recent excavation has revealed. At any rate Artemis Brauronia was honoured with a sacred enclosure on the Acropolis itself.

Artemis, who, to judge from her popularity as a subject for early Greek artists, was regarded as a major deity in archaic times, was also worshipped at the Elaphebolia—Deer shooting—a hunting festival held in March. The victims were harts or stags or offerings made to represent them.

Reference has been made to Hephaestus and his association with Athena both in ritual and myth. As god of subterranean fires his festival—the Hephaestia—included a torch-race. It must have provided a brilliant spectacle on a clear Greek night, and Herodotus likens the chains of runners to the relays of horsemen which carried messages across the Persian empire. A torch-light procession was also held in honour of Prometheus, the kindly Titan, who bestowed the gift of fire on men. The importance of fire and its conservation in a primitive community is obvious. But Prometheus was also revered as the chief of craftsmen, who, according to one legend, made men from clay. Probably his worship preceded that of Hephaestus in Attica. But as early as the sixth century their rites and functions were becoming identified.

The heroes too had their festivals in Attica. Heracles, the Greek Samson, whose antecedents ascend into Mycenaean times, was associated in particular with a local spot called Cynosarges where he had a precinct in the sixth century B.C. He was also honoured at Marathon, and according to the ancient authorities many other festivals were held in his honour. He was worshipped both under the cult title of Alexikakos—Defender from evil— and Melon—Apple. Apples would appear an unlikely sort of offering to be made to a demi-god of Heracles' fame, but the custom was naïvely explained as follows. The ox which was to be sacrificed to him ran away, so apples were substituted to represent its main features, two for its horns and four for its legs.

The national hero Theseus, whose great historical achievement was the unity of Attica under one capital Athens, was honoured with a shrine near the Agora at least from Pisistratus' time. His festival, the Theseia, was in origin a tribal feast, and the chief participants were drawn from the families who claimed direct descent from the hero or the children he saved from the Minotaur. As offerings of milk and honey were made at heroes' tombs, the rites of the Theseia were presumably partly chthonian. Later, in the fifth century, when the alleged bones of Theseus were brought back to Athens from the island of Scyros, the Theseia became a national feast. It was preceded, we are told, by a festival held in memory of the Amazons, the legendary warrior women, who were defeated in battle near Marathon. But as H. J. Rose pertinently observes: 'In general, there was a strong tendency, perhaps especially among antiquarians, to explain nameless monuments and festivals whose original meaning had been forgotten by relating them to this event.'

Immediately below the north wall of the Acropolis on the edge of the Agora stood the Anakeion—the shrine of the Princes—a cult title of the Dioscuri, which had been established there at least from Pisistratus' time. The divine twins, Castor and Pollux, sons of Leda, wife of Tyndareus, king of Sparta, were revered particularly in Dorian states, that is to say among the people who were the latest comers to Greece, retained the original broad A instead of using the long Ionic E, and inhabited, in the main, the Peloponnese and some islands. It was an old belief that one of any given pair of twins was immortal, and legend told how Leda was loved by Zeus on the same night as she was loved by Tyndareus with the result that one of her twins, Polydeuces—better known in his Latin form Pollux—was immortal and the other, Castor, mortal. The pair roamed the countryside performing heroic deeds until Castor fell in battle. Zeus then took pity on Polydeuces' grief and permitted both to share half the year in the world above, when they continued their adventurous careers, and six months in the world below.

A sinister story was told concerning them and the poet Simonides who was born near the middle of the sixth century. A certain rich man hired the poet to compose an ode in his honour. Simonides in order to embellish it included an exploit by the Dioscuri. Instead of being honoured by the reference the rich man paid the poet only part of his fee, curtly informing him that the Dioscuri could pay the rest. He did, however, have the good manners to invite Simonides to dinner. During the course of the meal a slave brought the news that two strange young men were waiting outside and wished to see the poet. When the latter came out he found no one, but at that precise moment the roof fell in, crushing the host and his assembled guests. There is something elemental and terrifying about the Dioscuri. They rode on white horses, were terrible fighters (especially Polydeuces who was an invincible boxer), were connected with the sea, and through it with the constellations. Obviously Athens could not afford to ignore such a powerful pair, particularly as one of their major functions was to protect mariners. We know nothing of the ritual performed in their honour, though women were elsewhere barred from their shrine.

As the visitor approached the splendid new portals, which the Pisistratids had built to grace the Acropolis, he observed on their right the sanctuary of the Charites. In early times the Charites or Graces were spirits of fertility and not originally three. They were in particular connected with flowers, as their names, variously given, seem to imply. Aglaia meant 'Radiance', Auxo, 'Increaser', Euphrosyne, 'Joy', Kale, 'Beautiful', and Thaleia 'Blooming'. Their worship was widespread in Greece even in archaic times. The ancient statue of Apollo at Delos, made by the sixth century sculptors Angelion and Tektaios, held a bow in its left hand and, if Pfeiffer is right, to symbolize the god's graciousness, the three Charites in its right. This contention gains support from the appearance of the Charites standing next to Apollo on the famous archaic masterpiece, the François Vase, which dates from 560 B.C. In Aristotle's time they were already associated with the other meaning of 'charis', viz. 'favour' or 'gratitude', and statues of benefactors with decrees in their honour were placed in their precinct. But in the sixth century their association, like that of so many deities, was nearer the earth, of whose floral bounty they were the formal expression.

Near the sanctuary of the Charites was the precinct of Hecate surnamed Epipyrgidia—'of the Bastion'—because it shared that rocky eminence with the temple of Athena Nike. The worship of this sinister chthonian goddess, who was represented in art as a triple image, associated with witchcraft and uncanny places like cross-roads, and received sacrifice of hounds, probably reached Athens during the sixth century. In Hesiod her functions are as universal as those of Athena, and include law and child-rearing, as well as the bringing of victory. In Athens her more primitive aspects appear to have prevailed, for, as Aristophanes tells us, meals of dogs' flesh were put out at cross-roads for her to devour.

Outside the Dipylon Gate, beside the stream Eridanus, was the sanctuary of the mysterious Tritopatores or Tritopatreis, if the two were originally identical, whose name seems to mean 'great-grandfathers', and who were perhaps the ancestral spirits worshipped by the Athenian clans. According to one authority prayers were offered to them on behalf of the children of the family. According to another they were wind-spirits, and so presumably connected with Orphic myth. Elderkin again interpreted their name as meaning 'those who have Triton for father', i.e. to say mermen, and connected them with Athena who was known to Homer as 'Tritogeneia', 'Triton-born', whatever the title implies. Clearly the Tritopatores were associated with water, as the proximity of their shrine to the Eridanus seems to prove, but Elderkin's subsequent identification of them with Erichthonius, Erechtheus and Cecrops on the ground that they were represented as anguiform in art is, to say the least, highly speculative. Whatever their origin, and they appear to have been benevolent ancestor spirits of some kind, the Tritopatores were typical of the many lesser cults with strong local roots which flourished in Athens in the sixth century. They were worshipped at Marathon too on the eve of the Skirophoria, the important fertility festival held in honour of Demeter, the Corn goddess, and her daughter.

One of the commonest sights in ancient Athens were the bronze or marble pillars, complete with bearded heads and genitals, generally known as 'herms'. They were furnished with 'arms' for wreaths to hang on, and were treated with the most signal respect. Indeed when they were mutilated at the time of the Sicilian expedition Athenian religious sentiment was outraged as never before. Hermes, god of wayfarers and good-luck, guider of the dead, and ultimately perhaps the spirit inhabiting dolmens or heaps of stones, had fertility associations, as his underworld rôle suggests, and being in a sense a dolmen could be represented in aniconic form. But the characteristic Greek tendency to represent everything in human terms would not be denied, though in this instance, as in the parallel case of Apollo Aguieus, it was halted, as it were, half way. We are told that a famous archaic herm which graced the Agora was universally admired as a work of art, but when or why the custom arose of setting herms up before the doors of houses is unknown, though Pausanias claimed that the Athenians invented it.

At the end of the century the younger Pisistratus erected an altar to the Twelve gods, i.e. to all the chief deities of the pantheon, in the Agora. It was commonly regarded as a place of sanctuary, like all altars and temples of the gods. But its very impersonality marked it out as something of an entirely different order from the highly individualized local cults. Yet one of these at least rising from humble beginnings was destined to achieve world renown.

NOTES TO CHAPTER II

Page 40. Phya. Cf. Herodotus, I, 60; Beloch, *Rhein.Mus.*, XLV.

41. Old Temple. Cf. Dinsmoor, *AJA*, 1947, pp. 109–51.

Erechtheus. Cf. Iliad, II, 547; Odyssey, VII, 81; Farnell, *GHC*, p. 11; *CGS*, I, p. 393; IV, pp. 47–52.

Athena. Cf. Nilsson, *Geschichte*[2], I, pp. 346 ff.; Palmer, *The Interpretation of Mycenaean Greek Texts*, p. 239.

42. Pharaoh. The word originally meant 'palace'. Cf. Gardiner, *Egypt of the Pharaohs*, p. 52.

Holy Acropolis. Cf. Travlos, *Exelixis*, p. 42.

Erechtheum. Cf. Herodotus, VIII, 55.

Butes. Cf. Farnell, *CGS*, I, pp. 58, 91; and Elderkin's speculative account in *Studies in Early Athenian Cult*, III (Classical Studies presented to Edward Capps. pp. 114 ff).

43. Snake. Cf. Herodotus, VIII, 41.

Original Parthenon. Cf. Dinsmoor, ibid., and for an opposed view Plommer, *JHS*, LXXX, 1960, pp. 140 ff.

44. Panathenaea. Cf. Davison, *JHS*, LXXVIII, 1958, pp. 23 ff.; Corbett, P. E., *JHS*, LXXX, 1960, pp. 57 ff.

Arrephoroi (and subsequent accounts of festivals), Deubner, *AF* pp. 9 ff.

45. Harmodius and Aristogeiton. Cf. Thucydides, VI, 56.

Plynteria. Cf. Xenophon, *Hell.*, I, 4, 12; Plutarch, *Alcib.*, 34.

46. Dorians. Cf. Herodotus, V, 72.

Korai. Cf. D'Ooge, *Acropolis of Athens*, pp. 96–7; Payne & Young, pp. 14 ff.

47. Older Parthenon. Cf. Dinsmoor, *AJA*, 1934, 405; *AAG*, 149. Moods of Old Temple and Parthenon. Cf. Herington, *Athena Parthenos and Athena Polias*; Parthenos & Parthenon, *G&R*, supp. 1963.

48. Chalkeia. Cf. Sophocles, *fgm.* 77.

Aegis. Cf. Farnell, *CGS*, I, pp. 96 ff.

49. Semnai. Cf. Sophocles, *OC*, 90, 458; Paus. I, 28, 6.

Ares. Cf. Euripides, *Electra*, pp. 1258 ff.

Areopagus. Cf. Hignett, *A History of the Athenian Constitution*, p. 80.

House of Arrephoroi. Cf. Hill, *Ancient City of Athens*, p. 178.

Arrephoroi. Cf. Pausanias, I, 27, 3.

50. Aphrodite. Cf. Pausanias, I, 19, 2; Broneer, *Hesperia*, 1935, pp. 125 ff.

Aglauros. Cf. Rose, H. J., *A Handbook of Greek Mythology*, p. 111.

51. Old Athens. Cf. Thucydides, II, 15.

Olympieion. Aristotle, *Pol.*, 1313B; Wycherley, *GRBS*, 1964.

Zeus. Cf. Judeich, *Topographie²*, pp. 257, 276, 283; Wycherley, ibid.

52. Dipoleia. Cf. Pausanias, I, 24, 4.

Pandia. Cf. Frazer, *Pausanias*, II, pp. 303–4.

53. Diasia. Cf. Thucydides, I, 126, 6.

54. Wooden Image. Cf. Pausanias, I, 3, 5.

Kronos. Cf. Walcot, 'The Text of Hesiod's Theogony and the *Hittite Epic of Kumarbi*', *CQ*, 1956, pp. 198 ff.

55. Pythian Apollo. Cf. Thucydides, II, 15; Euripides, *Ion*, 938; Strabo, IX, 2, 11; Wycherley, *The Pythion at Athens*, *AJA*, 1963, pp. 75 ff.

Pisistratus the Younger. Cf. Thucydides, VI, 55.

Apollo Patroos. Cf. Pausanias, I, 3, 4.

56. Pharmakoi. Cf. Aristophanes, *Frogs*, 733.

   Eiresione. Cf. Aristophanes, *Knights*, 728 f.

57. Boedromia. Cf. Aeschylus, *Persians*, 393; Aristophanes, *Acharnians*, 1213.

   Apollo Aguieus. Cf. Nilsson, *Geschichte*[2], 1, pp. 562 ff.

   Brauron. Cf. Herodotus, VI, 138; Madame Kahil, Lecture to the Académie des Inscriptions, reported in the *Guardian*, March 7, 1964.

   Bears. For their continued existence in Greece, cf. Fermor, *Mani*, p. 269.

58. Offerings to Artemis. Cf. Herbillon, *Cultes de Patras*, pp. 55 ff.

   Hephaestus. Cf. Herodotus, VIII, 98.

59. Cynosarges. Cf. Herodotus, V, 63; VI, 116.

   Theseus. Cf. Ath. Pol., 15, 4; Pausanias, I, 17, 2.

60. Simonides. Cf. Phaedrus, 4, 25.

   Pisistratid Portals. Cf. Dinsmoor, *AJA*, 1947, pp. 119 and 148.

   Charites. Cf. Pausanias, IX, 35, 2; Aristotle, *Eth. Nic.*, 1133A.

   Delian Apollo. Cf. Pfeiffer, 'The Image of the Delian Apollo', *Journal of the Warburg and Courtauld Institute*, XV, 1952; Webster in *Fifty Years of Classical Scholarship*, pp. 88 ff.

61. Hecate. Hesiod, *Theogony*, 411 f.; Homeric, *Hymn to Demeter*, 52 f.; Aristophanes, *Plutus*, 594 f.; Fontenrose, *Cult and Myth of Pyrrhos at Delphi*, p. 238.

   Tritopatores. Cf. Deubner, *AF*, p. 44; Elderkin, ibid.

62. Hermes and Herms. Cf. Pausanias, I, 15, 1; Chittenden, *Hesperia*, XVI, 1947, pp. 89 ff.; *AJA*, 1948, pp. 24 ff.; Wycherley, *Testimonia*, Nos. 305 and 308.

   Twelve gods. Cf. Wycherley, *CQ*, IV, 1954, pp. 143–50.

CHAPTER III

THE ELEUSINIAN MYSTERIES

The Homeric Hymn to Demeter, which appears to date from about 600 B.C., has been thought to preserve in epic form much of the ritual of the Mysteries. It describes how Aidoneus, better known as Hades, the 'Unseen', a euphemistic title of Death, could find no one willing to share his grisly kingdom. Spying Persephone, Demeter's daughter, gathering flowers in company with the Oceanids in the plain of Nysa, he ensnared her with a lovely bloom and bore her away beneath the earth. Demeter's grief was so inconsolable that the world grew barren and Zeus was moved to restore the girl to her mother. Aidoneus dare not refuse his great brother's request, but even Zeus was powerless in face of the law which laid down that return from the underworld was only possible for those who had eaten nothing there. Persephone unfortunately had eaten some pomegranate seeds, so a compromise was agreed whereby she was permitted to return to earth for eight months only before rejoining her consort among the shades. Demeter meantime had wandered to Eleusis, and been kindly treated by king Celeus. In return she attempted to render his infant son invulnerable by burning him in the fire, but was surprised by the child's mother, who spoiled her plan. Thereupon the angry goddess revealed herself in all her dread majesty and commanded the Eleusinians to raise a temple and altar in her honour by the spring of Kallichoron.

The myth as recorded, and apparently also by the nebulous Pamphos, if Pausanias really used him to check his own account, is compound of three elements. One, and possibly the earliest, was concerned with the chthonian deity, connected with agriculture and fertility, variously known as Plutus or Pluto, whose name means 'Wealthy', presumably in the specialized sense of riches in the earth. That he should have in the course of time become identified with Hades, and his wife with Persephone, who were also associated with the depths below, is scarcely surprising, if such in fact was the true course of events. Why the equation should have been made at Eleusis we do not know, unless the Hymn was composed as a piece of propaganda either in the Eleusinian or the Athenian cause. Eleusis at any rate possessed the Rharian plain, where the science of agriculture was supposed to have been first practised, as well as a hero of the stature of Triptolemus who was destined to attain wide fame. Super-imposed upon or coeval with the legend of Pluto/Hades and Persephone was the worship of the corn-goddess Demeter and her daughter Kore—the word means 'maiden' or 'daughter'—who was apparently a personification of the seed-corn which, as Nilsson suggested, was kept in subterranean silos after the harvest until the period of the autumn sowing. This barren season was described in myth as the time of Kore's absence in the under-world. Finally the story of how the local Eleusinian king adopted the worship of Demeter may have an historical basis in Mycenaean times.

At the beginning of the sixth century B.C. the sanctuary at Eleusis, like that at Delphi, was far smaller and simpler than it afterwards became. The ancient temple of Demeter was then re-placed by a modest Telesterion or Hall of Initiation, built prob-ably at the instance of Solon when the city came finally into Athens' sphere of influence, and the Mysteries were recognized by law. It measured only 18·37 by 14 m as against the fifth century structure of Coroebus which was more than 50 metres square. Within it stood the Anaktoron, or 'King's Shrine', which had occupied relatively the same position both in the archaic temple and in its predecessor the Mycenaean megaron, where the 'hiera' or 'sacred objects' were kept. There was also built at this time a successor to the so-called 'Sacred House', where religious rites of an unspecified nature took place, involv-ing an altar, and offerings of pottery and figurines. About the sacred well of Kallichoron, mentioned in the Hymn, dances took place in honour of Demeter, watched from a raised base, and worship took place at a much revered and carefully preserved altar.

By the time of Pisistratus the fame of the Mysteries had spread far and wide through the Greek-speaking world, and it became necessary to enlarge the Telesterion in order to accommodate the growing number of candidates for initiation. The propaganda value of a festival which attracted foreigners, including barbarians before the Persian Wars, was naturally not lost upon a tyrant anxious to impress the world with Athens' might and glory, so no expense seems to have been spared upon the new shrine. The Pisistratean Telesterion, like its fifth century successor, was square, though only half the size. It was nevertheless a magnificent improvement on the Solonian edifice, with its noble columns, marble sima and Dorian entablature. It was evidently a work of great artistic merit as may be judged from the considerable remains. The Anaktoron occupied the south-west corner, and though small was large enough to contain the sacred objects and the Hierophant or 'Revealer of the Mysteries'. In an adjacent court stood the twin altars of the goddesses, where the various officials swore oaths. More primitive and sinister than the rest was the Ploutonion, or cave of Pluto, which contained a small temple, also dating from Pisistratean times. Such was the setting for a festival which was destined to achieve even greater importance than the Panathenaea, and the reason why it did so is perhaps not far to seek. The sixth century B.C. was a period of remarkable religious ferment when the ordinary individual, who enjoyed no gentile privilege, was becoming more and more concerned about the after-life. The Isles of the Blest were reserved for heroes and those favoured by the gods, or what usually amounted to the same thing, by birth, for Homer had no care for the common man's soul. The initiation ceremony at Eleusis, impressive and satisfying by its very nature, seemed to proffer some real hope, and for those who returned death had apparently lost much of its terror. It seems strange, of course, that a belief in future immortality could grow out of a humble ritual connected with a fertile patch of land, or some long forgotten palace ceremony involving, as in the case of Athena and Erechtheus, a goddess and a king. Yet so it was, and although the details of the Mysteries have remained a secret some general notions may be gleaned about them from the reports of witnesses in various ages. Unfortunately, no literary evidence, apart from the Hymn, survives from the archaic period, and the rest must be used with caution even for the ages which they describe. A possible reconstruction of the order of events, based on Mylonas, might be as follows:

On the 14th of Boedromion, our September, a band of ephebes, armed youths from Athens, was despatched to Eleusis, a distance of fourteen miles, to escort the holy objects, kept in the Anaktoron, back to the city. The latter which were clearly of only modest size and weight were carried in boxes by priestesses, proceeding on foot, and delivered at the archaic Eleusinion. On the following day, called Agyrmos, or Day of Assembly, the King Archon summoned the people to hear the proclamation announcing the festival, probably near the site of the future Painted Stoa, where it was delivered in later times. The proclamation was read out by the Hierokeryx or Holy Herald, a member of the family of Kerykes who claimed the privilege by ancestral right, in the presence of the Hierophant, who belonged to the even more important Eleusinian family of the Eumolpidae, and the Dadouchos, or Bearer of the Torch. The purpose of the proclamation was apparently to warn all such as were ritually impure that they could not be accepted as candidates for initiation, though foreigners and even barbarians were not debarred on that account, providing they spoke Greek.

On the 16th came the injunction 'Seaward Mystai' and everyone proceeded to Phalerum or the Piraeus to wash away contagion in the brine. With them they took pigs which, after undergoing like the candidates ritual immersion, were sacrificed probably that evening.

Next day solemn sacrifice was offered to Demeter and Kore, probably at the Eleusinion, by the Archon assisted by the *Paredros*, or Deputy Director, and the four *Epimeletae* or Overseers, two of whom, like the Hierophant, were members of the Eumolpidae. Then came a day of rest for the candidates, while special preparations were made to deal with late-comers who had missed the preliminary sacrifices. It was later honoured by the title of Asclepius himself, who was a late-comer from Epidaurus to Athens.

On the 19th the grand procession headed by the wooden image of Iacchus, a personification of the ritual cry 'Iacchus, O Iacchus', accompanied by its special priest the *Iacchagogos*, set out for Eleusis to restore the hiera to their rightful home, and to undergo initation in the Telesterion. Behind the *Iacchagogos* came the priestesses bearing the hiera in the boxes, together with the Hierophant in his myrtle crown, the other priests and officiants, state representatives, and finally the Mystae, both men and women, and the non-Athenian citizens accompanied by their sponsors. Children were also included, and one of them, elected by lot, was despatched 'from the hearth' to be initiated by the state.

The mood and deportment of the throng as it wound slowly along the Sacred Way was probably not so solemn as might have been expected, but rather that of holiday. Certainly there must have been much good-humoured badinage at the bridges, whether when crossing the local Cephisus, or the river so-named at Eleusis, when men with heads covered hurled abuse, to ward off evil, at the important personages passing below. That this custom was old is clear from the reference in the Homeric Hymn to the maiden Iambe—literally 'Abuse'—who alone succeeded in making the mourning Demeter smile.

Frequent halts would have been made at the numerous shrines passed en route, some of which may still be seen by modern visitors travelling by car or bus. On the Cephisus stood the shrine, sacred to the two goddesses, where the hero Phytalus—the name means 'Planter'—had entertained Demeter during her wanderings and received in return a fig-tree as a gift. Further on was an altar of Zeus Meilichios, who, being like Demeter concerned with fertility, would also have been honoured by the procession moving by. The temple of Kyamites—Bean-Man—was of special significance as beans were a popular article of diet in Greece, and the cult, despite Pausanias' denial that Demeter could have had anything to do with it, may well have been founded under the influence of Eleusis. In the pass below Mount Aigaleos lay Daphnai, once a convent and formerly a shrine of Apollo, and beyond it again the temple of Aphrodite. Skirting the Thriasian plain the weary travellers viewed at last Eleusis' towering citadel, hard by the narrow gulf where Xerxes' fleet was destined to perish. Climbing the hill above the Rheitoi, the brackish pools which lay alongside the shore, the Mystae tied saffron-hued fillets to alternate hands and legs in the rite known as Krokosis, performed in honour of the hero Krokon. In archaic times it seems doubtful whether the Mystae, whose advent, according to Herodotus, was heralded by a cloud of dust, wore special clothes for the procession. That they were in festive array was sufficiently obvious from their myrtle-crowns, cornsheaves and woollen-bound *bacchoi*, as well as the long knotted staves on which they slung their bundles. The latter presumably contained clean robes for the ceremony, together with blankets and articles of a more personal nature. Beyond the Rheitoi reared Eumolpus' tomb, eponymous hero of the priestly clan which controlled the festival, and soon appeared the grim Ploutonion which was locally regarded as the scene of Kore's abduction.

That night the pilgrims rested while the women performed the Kernophoria, balancing pots on their myrtle-wreathed heads and solemnly circling the 'Fount of Fair Dances'. Everyone was then charged by the Mystagogoi to observe a partial fast in memory of Demeter, abstaining from wine and various foods until they had drunk the kykeon. This was a posset of barley-meal and mint, consumed while seated on a ram's fleece. It was apparently followed, though the precise sequence of events is hard to determine, by an official sacrifice controlled by the Archon Basileus and the lesser officials as well as ephebes, and the offering of a cake made from corn harvested on the Rharian plain. Finally the concourse entered the sacred enclosure.

The Teletai or Mystery rites apparently included three main elements, viz. *Dromena*—Things performed, *Legomena*—Things said, and *Deiknumena*—Things shown. Of these we know nothing as the Mystae were sworn to secrecy, but something may perhaps be hazarded concerning their nature in the light of the Hymn and such evidence as has survived. The *Dromena* could have been a pageant performed within the sacred enclosure, representing Demeter's search for her daughter. Indeed that such performances were not unknown may be gleaned, as will appear, from the Lesser Mysteries. The *Legomena* were presumably ritual utterances of some kind or other, but as little credence can be placed in Hesychius the lexicographer's meaningless 'Pax, Konx' password as in Christian Clement of Alexandria's formula: 'I fasted and drank the kykeon; I took from the box, and having performed [or tasted, if we accept Lobeck's emendation] I put into the basket and from the basket into the box.' The supreme moment of the initiation ceremony was not concerned with ritual, as Mylonas rightly insists, but with the *Deiknumena*—the Things shown. Suddenly the doors of the Anaktoron swung open to emit a blaze of light, streaming presumably from the torch of the Dadouchos, as the Hierophant revealed the Hiera. Alongside him stood the goddess' holy priestess and the two hierophantides, female 'expounders of the mysteries', representing Demeter and her daughter. The effect must have been as awe-inspiring as the moment when the Orthodox bishop proclaims the Resurrection of Christ.

The nature of the Orgia is much disputed, and will almost certainly be never resolved. Possibly they were Mycenaean cult objects, as Mylonas suggests, whose provenance and purpose had been long forgotten. Possibly again the parable of the cycle of vegetation played its part, though we can hardly accept Hippolytus' contemptuous statement that the *Epoptae* or Adepts, who were admitted to the higher mysteries, were merely shown a ripe ear of wheat. According to the same authority the ritual also included a holy birth. 'In the course of the night,' he says, 'the hierophant at Eleusis in the midst of a brilliant fire celebrating the Great and Unspoken Mysteries cries and shouts aloud saying "Holy Brimo has borne a sacred child Brimos, that is the Mighty has given birth to the Mighty One".'

The account of the fire, as Mylonas observes, derives from Plutarch, but the remainder of the statement must raise grave suspicions emanating as it does from a non-Initiate. At the same time it seems hard to credit that the incident of the child in the Homeric Hymn was entirely ignored in the ceremony. Possibly it formed part of the Dromena or pageant, if Mylonas' guess is correct, or possibly there was some ritual birth in connection with Kore, to whom the title Brimo was applied, as well as to Deo in the Mysteries of Rhea-Cybele mentioned by Clement.

On the other hand there seems no reason to connect the incident of Iambe, which was presumably commemorated in the *Gephyrismoi*, with the bawdy story of Baubo, which as Mylonas notes, had striking features in common with the Egyptian festival at Bubastis. Indeed all obscenities imputed to the Mysteries by Christian apologists are naturally open to question. Finally the Initiates performed the rite of *Plemochoai* pouring libations to the dead, before abandoning themselves to dancing and singing in the mood of men reborn. Next day they walked back to Athens filled with enthusiasm for what they had endured. Such were the Greater Mysteries which were Eleusis' gift to Athens.

A necessary preliminary to the Greater Mysteries, if we may judge from a parallel offered by Plato, were the Lesser Mysteries

held at Agrai in Attica on the Ilissus in the month of Anthesterion
—February. They were traditionally founded in honour of
Heracles, but were probably an independent Attic creation
established, as Farnell suggested, out of rivalry with Eleusis,
when the latter was still closed to outsiders. They were apparently sacred to Kore only, and only incidentally to her mother, a
circumstance which the season of the year might help to explain
as in February in Greece the young corn is beginning to shoot.
They were apparently held sometimes twice a year in order to
give those who had missed the February festival an opportunity to
obtain preliminary initiation in time for the main ordeal in September. Of the details of the festival we know virtually nothing,
and no archaeological remains survive. Stephanus' statement that
there was 'an imitation of the representations held in honour of
Dionysus' is well taken by Mylonas, following Goudis, as implying that the festival included a pageant, concerned presumably
with the myths of Kore, like the theatrical performances held in
the theatre.

At Athens certain women's festivals were concerned either
directly or indirectly with Demeter. Most famous was the
Thesmophoria which was confined to married women, and was
held in the middle of Pyanepsion, the month of the Bean-Boiling,
our October/November. As it was known to Herodotus we may
assume that it existed in the previous century, although the details are preserved for the most part in late authorities who tend to
confuse them with those of allied feasts. They bear at any rate
the appearance of great antiquity and are concerned with the
fertility of the earth.

The preliminary part, known as the Stenia, took place at night,
when the women assembled to indulge in mutual vilification and
language which by its very grossness was best calculated to scare
off evil influences, like the *Gephyrismoi*—the Abuse from the
Bridges—during the procession to Eleusis. Next day they celebrated the Anodos—the 'Ascent'—in procession to the Thesmo-
phorion, a shrine which may have been situated in the region of
the Pnyx though its precise location is quite uncertain. This was
followed by the Nesteia or Fasting when they all abstained from
food and wine, like Demeter in her sorrow, as well as from sexual
indulgence. Then they constructed bowers of branches and
squatted on the ground before breaking their fast on a meal of

roast pork, the goddess' sacred animal. The fast was presumably undertaken in order to preserve their powers of fertility in the belief that by so doing they would produce a like reaction in the earth. The bowers again and squatting were clearly intended to bring them into close physical contact with the soil.

On the final day, called Kalligeneia, 'Bearer of Fair Offspring', solemn intercession was made for the promotion of the fertility of the corn crops as well as for that of mankind. The rotting remains of the pigs which had been sacrificed at the Skira were now exhumed and mixed with the corn which was due to be sown.

So much may be reasonably inferred concerning the Thesmophoria from whose celebration all men were firmly banned. Some authorities claim that it included a dance and mime, presumably concerning the Rape of Kore, similar to the one performed at Halimus on the coast. Others, like Frazer, have read some esoteric significance into the term 'Anodos', interpreting it in the light of the myth as the 'Coming Up' of Kore. Though such interpretations have been dismissed as fanciful it seems quite possible that all kinds of symbolic meanings were attached to the rites in later times. But in the sixth century B.C. when the festivals had still to attain their classical forms the emphasis was probably on fertility ritual regarded mainly from a pragmatic point of view. The very name Thesmophoria seems to mean 'Bringing of the Treasures' (of the earth), a rare and presumably ancient sense of *thesmos* which occurs only in the sixth century lyric poet Anacreon.

The Skira was celebrated on the twelfth of the month presumably named after it, that is to say June/July. The word, we are told, was used for offerings like sucking-pigs and edible objects in snake or phallic form. The time was the end of the old Attic year when the corn was ready to be reaped, and the earth's vitality all but spent. Then it was felt was the appropriate season to reinvigorate the land's waning powers by offerings of objects evocative of fertility. The pigs were sacrificed and the offerings were poured into pits called *megara*, to be consumed by the earth through the medium of snakes. This custom was commemorated in the myth about Eubouleus the swine-herd—'Good-Counsellor' being a euphemistic title of Hades himself—who lost his pigs when the chasm opened and swallowed Kore.

For the duration of the festival the women practised sexual abstention, and to cool men's ardour chewed garlic to counteract their perfume. That is all we know. The details were further confused with a festival of Athena Skiras whose worship had been imported from Salamis, and with the custom of shading the priestess of Athena Polias and the priests of Poseidon and Helios under an awning—skiron—while proceeding to a place called Skiron near the city. What seems clear is that the Skira was in origin a primitive agricultural ritual concerned with the fertility of the earth. In modern times we are less concerned with the success of the harvest than the ancients as we can buy corn abroad. But Attica depended for its bread on the niggardly produce of its own poor soil, so that any ritual which bid fair to increase its doubtful fertility was eagerly practised at the appropriate season. Pigs were sacred to Demeter, and being highly fertile animals their numerous progeny made cheap and suitable objects for sacrifice to subterranean powers. The snake again symbolized the mysterious forces of the earth, while the phallos was the most obvious sign of potency. Even in modern times, according to Deubner, peasants in Herzogovina sketched phalloi on their fields in the hope of thereby inducing potency in the soil.

The Haloa, which was the ancient equivalent of the Harvest Home, was celebrated in Posideon, our December. Like the Thesmophoria and Skira it was reserved for women, though the demarch assisted at Eleusis, and archons after setting out wine and tables escorted the participants to the place of ritual from which they themselves were rigorously excluded. There was apparently much licence and jesting and, if we can believe the evidence of the corrupt Lucian scholium, eating of confections in sexual shapes. But too little is known about the precise details of any of the festivals to claim certainty on any specific point. They were all doubtless agrarian festivals in origin which steadily gained prominence during the sixth century B.C. until they finally attained national status. Deubner's claim that they included much ritual obscenity is not on the evidence certain. Indeed how far phallic rites constituted an original feature of any of these festivals is difficult to assess. Their prominence in other celebrations, and in particular in the Rural Dionysia, may have led to borrowing or imitation on a considerable scale, or they may have been a feature of all primitive agrarian feasts.

The theory that there is some intimate relationship between women and agriculture has been doubtfully proved. At Pheneos in Arcadia, as Farnell noted, it was a priest who celebrated the rites of Demeter Cidaria by beating on the earth, and it was to men, not women, that the Mysteries were revealed both in the Argolid and at Eleusis. At the same time there is no denying that the deities of fertility, whether Athena, Hera or Demeter herself, were normally goddesses, though male divinities like Pan, Priapus at Lampsacus on the Hellespont, and Hermes were not unknown. So if sympathetic magic was to be tried on the earth its chances of success must have appeared considerably heightened if the active participants were fertile in themselves.

Whether the festivals here mentioned all originated in Eleusis is difficult to say. Certainly with the annexation of the city at the end of the seventh century the fame of the Corn-goddess was spread abroad. Doubtless too her cult came then to embrace many independent agrarian rituals which were modified in her honour and came to be regarded as her own. She also came to be associated or identified with grim and bestial deities in regions outside Attica. Notable among these was the wooden horse-headed Demeter, known as 'the Black', who was worshipped in a cave at Phigaleia. The antiquity of the cult is not absolutely proved by the 'xoanon', though few such images could have been carved in later times. 'The head and the hair were those of a horse,' says Pausanias, 'and attached to the head were snakes and wild beasts.' Myths were also extant at Thelpousa which connected Demeter with Poseidon, the old interpretation of whose name as 'lord of the earth' seems to be supported by Mycenaean evidence. Poseidon was said to have mated with her in horse form, when she had changed herself into a mare in order to escape his attentions. She was also surnamed Erinys, though for no obvious reason, except perhaps that she could occasion famine as easily as plenty. Despoina, the Mistress, a hieratic title of Persephone, was also said to have been her daughter by Poseidon, though she is not connected with Artemis or her forebears in legend.

But the local cults of Demeter were not uniformly grim. We are told that Cypselus, tyrant of Corinth during the seventh century B.C., instituted beauty contests in the plain of the Alpheius and dedicated a precinct and altar to Demeter of Eleusis.

Though the figure of Triptolemus, to whom in the Hymn the goddess revealed the Mysteries, is a favourite in art from archaic times, he apparently had no place in the Mysteries themselves.

He belonged in the main to legend, though the existence of his temple and threshing floor on the Rharian plain suggests that he was in origin, like Echetlaeus or Kyamites, a rustic hero. It was natural that he should be drawn into association with the two goddesses, and become a symbol of Attic supremacy in agriculture and the arts.

NOTES TO CHAPTER III

Page 65. Homeric Hymn to Demeter. Cf. Mylonas, *The Hymn to Demeter and her Sanctuary at Eleusis*, pp. 15 ff.

Pamphos. Cf. Pausanias, I, 38, 3; I, 39, 1.

Plutus, Pluto. Cf. Nilsson, *Geschichte*[2], I, p. 471.

66. Archaeology of Eleusis. Cf. Mylonas, *Eleusis and the Eleusinian Mysteries* (with notes); Travlos, *Archaiologikon Deltion*, 1961–2.

Kallichoron. Cf. Hymn, 272.

68. Eleusinion. Cf. Pausanias, I, 14, 1; Wycherley, *Athenian Agora III, Testimonia*, pp. 74–85; Thompson, *Hesperia*, 1960, p. 334.

Kerykes. Cf. Ferguson, *Hesperia*, 7, 1938, p. 23.

Barbarians. Cf. Farnell, *CGS*, III, 155.

Asclepius. Cf. Pausanias, II, 26, 8; Edelstein, *Asclepius*, II, p. 127.

Iacchus. Cf. Aristophanes, *Frogs*, 340–50; Pausanias, I, 2, 4.

69. Children. Cf. Farnell, op. cit., p. 164.

Iambe. Cf. Hymn, 202 f.

Heroes and Shrines. Cf. Pausanias, I, 37, 38.

Aphrodite, Cf. Travlos, *Praktika*, 1937, pp. 25–33.

Mystae. Cf. Herodotus, VIII, 65.

70. Kykeon. Cf. Hymn, 49, 200–1, 208 ff. Cf. also Iliad, XI, 624, 641; Odyssey, X, 234, 316.

71. Baubo. Cf. Guthrie, *Orpheus*, pp. 135 ff.

Lesser Mysteries. Cf. Plato, *Republic*, II, 364E; Farnell, op. cit., p. 170; Hooker, 'Topography of the Frogs', *JHS*, LXXX, 1960, pp. 112 ff.

72. Thesmophoria. Cf. Herodotus, II, 171; Deubner, *AF*, pp. 50 ff.

73. Anodos. Cf. Frazer, *GB*, II, p. 299.

Thesmos. Cf. Anacreon, *fgm*. 58.

Skira. Cf. Deubner, op. cit., pp. 40 ff.

74. Haloa. Cf. Deubner, op. cit., pp. 66 ff.

75. Demeter Cidaria. Cf. Farnell, op. cit., pp. 107 & 112.

THE ELEUSINIAN MYSTERIES

Demeter Cults. Cf. Pausanias, VIII, 25, 4 f.; 42, 1 f.

Poseidon. Cf. Palmer, *The Interpretation of Mycenaean Greek Texts*, p. 256.

Beauty Contests. Cf. Athenaeus, XIII, 609F, quoting Nicias, the historian of Arcadia.

CHAPTER IV

DIONYSUS

❖

A famous vase-painting, by the late sixth century master Exekias, depicts Dionysus seated on ship-board, while a vine climbs up the mast and bunches of grapes overhang the deck. The god himself is ivy-crowned and bearded, and dolphins sport in the sea. The scene accords very closely with the description of his capture by Tyrrhenian pirates in the Homeric Hymn, except that in this case the god is alone.

> *And on a sudden a vine spread out along the sail-top this way and that, and many a bunch of grapes hung down——*

It seems curious at first to find Dionysus in a sea context as the evidence, such as it is, has seemed to suggest that his cult moved south from Thrace by land and finally reached Attica via Boeotia. Yet Apollo Delphinios reached Delphi by sea, and it is possible that one form of Dionysiac worship reached Athens from Ionia prior to the introduction of the cult, later associated with the City Dionysia, from neighbouring Eleutherae. The possibility is strengthened by the inclusion in Ionian celebrations of the Anthesteria of a *katagogia* or ritual 'bringing home' of the god's image, apparently on a waggon or a vehicle fashioned like a ship. Such vehicles are familiar from Attic black-figured vase paintings of an earlier era, which show the god, or his image, riding along escorted by satyrs or celebrants. The context of these scenes cannot be proved with certainty, though it seems at least possible that they are somewhat fanciful representations of an actual procession of which the *katagogia* constituted an integral part. The probability that they are connected with the Athenian Anthesteria gains support from the discovery of a late inscription referring to the *katagogia* in connection with Iobacchos, a cult which there is reason to suppose superseded that of Dionysus in the Marshes. Thucydides mentions the latter in conjunction with the Olympieion, the Pythion, and the shrine of Ge as proof that the oldest part of the city outside the Acropolis lay to the south of the citadel. There, he says, 'the older Dionysia' were celebrated on the twelfth of Anthesterion. The reference is clearly to the Anthesteria, a very ancient festival with affinities dating from Mycenaean times.

The name of this festival has been interpreted, and usually misinterpreted, in many ways. There is, at any rate, a strong presumption that it was connected with flowers, which are just beginning to bloom in Greece in February, while Philistius' statement that it derived its title from the custom of the wearing by children of crowns of flowers is supported by the evidence from numerous jugs. Nevertheless its prime concern was with the jars of wine made from the previous autumn's vintage which were now duly broached and tasted. This was a serious ritual event as it was obviously of the first importance to gain the god's favour before venturing to enjoy the wine from the vintage for which he alone was responsible. This could best be done by making libation to him in his oldest seat of worship, and the degree of reverence which was attached to the act may be gauged from the extraordinary circumstance that the temple was never opened to the public except on this unique occasion.

We are told that on the opening day of the three-day festival, known as the *Pithoigia* or Jar-opening, the people assembled at the sanctuary of Dionysus in the Marshes, opened the jars containing the wine obtained from the previous autumn's vintage and made libation to the god. The rest of the day was passed in conviviality in celebration of the event. The next day was called the *Choes* or Jugs, when the conviviality continued and included a drinking match commemorating the entertainment offered Orestes before his trial for murder. Finally the revellers returned with their pots, ritually garlanded, and offered further libations in the presence of the priestess at the temple. Yet, according to other authorities, it was a day of ill-omen when the souls of the dead visited the upper world, and men chewed buckthorn and put pitch on their doors to discourage their visits. But possibly there was confusion with the *Chytroi*, the day following. There also took place within the sanctuary the secret ceremonies preparatory to the marriage of the wife of the Archon Basileus—the *Basilinna*—to Dionysus which was solemnized in the Boukolion. These were conducted by the fourteen priestesses, known as *Gerairai*, but of the details of the preparations or of the subsequent ceremony we are completely in the dark. At the same time the purpose of the sacred marriage is hardly in dispute. The citizens of Athens could expect to benefit in real terms from the ritual marriage arranged between the wife of their chief magistrate and the powerful fertility god. Probably the custom ascended to earlier times when the wife of the actual king was involved. Possibly it had nothing originally to do with Dionysus, but became attached to the exciting new worship which had one day arrived by sea. In this case the ceremony of the *katagogia* would have had an appropriate place in the procession of the *Basilinna* and the *Gerairai* to the Boukolion. The god's bull affinities, again, were doubtless remembered at the 'Ox-stall'. That the bull was sacred to Dionysus and that he himself was sometimes worshipped in bull form is clear from Aeschylus' reference to the 'imitations of bull-bellowings' as well as the doubtless ritualistic description in Homer of Lycurgus pursuing Dionysus and his nurses with an ox-goad. A similar legend again was told about Butes, while the inhabitants of Tenedos sacrificed a calf to Dionysus 'Man Destroyer'. The women of Elis again addressed the god as 'the worthy bull', and he was known as 'Ox-born' at Argos.

The possibility that the wheeled ship carrying Dionysus' image was filled with bands of revellers shouting abuse 'from the carts' is supported by some evidence, but whether the ribaldry was regarded as possessing any ritual significance or merely expressed high spirits there is no way of knowing. The third day of the Anthesteria is very mysterious and has provoked much controversy. It was called the *Chytroi* or 'Porridge Pots' and began on the evening of the *Choes*. But its mood, to judge from the authorities, was far from convivial. Indeed we are assured that it was a day of gloom and associated with the dead, who had perished in Deucalion's (the Greek Noah's) flood. Much has been made, in this latter connection, of the notorious trimeter, preserved by the lexicographers: 'Out of doors Carians [or Keres] the Anthesteria is over'. If the reading Carians be correct, then the saying may have represented a blunt warning to the slaves that the holiday was over. If, on the other hand, it represented an injunction to the dead to forsake the homes of the living then the incongruity of the attachment of such a festival to the Anthesteria can only be explained on one ground, namely that the last day of the celebrations happened to coincide with a separate festival of the dead which eventually became included in it. This possibility is strengthened by the mention of Hermes Chthonios by an ancient commentator on Aristophanes in connection with the *Chytroi*. On the other hand there is no mention of any expulsion of ghosts elsewhere in Athens, and it may be, as Pickard-Cambridge suggested, that confusion with the Roman Lemuria took place in later times. If we exclude this possibility, and the evidence, though late, for some form of chthonian festival is strong, then we must suppose that the transference to Dionysus took place in the sixth century B.C. when the god had become popular in a civic capacity, and was rendered the more natural by vestiges of an underworld tradition in connection with the god himself.

Plutarch tells us that comic *agones* took place on the day of the 'Porridge Pots', from which protagonists were selected for the performances at the City Dionysia. As these latter were held in the theatre of Dionysus, which only dates from the sixth century B.C., the *agones*, as Pickard-Cambridge rightly argues, could not have been included in the older Anthesteria, neither were they necessarily of a dramatic character.

The nature of the Anthesteria in archaic times is not, perhaps, difficult to reconstruct, at least in the form celebrated at Athens. In essence it was a thanksgiving for the fertility of the vine crop, and was of a humble and simple nature. During February the old Athenians gathered at the temple of Dionysus in the Marshes clutching their jars of last year's wine. After making libation to the deity who was its author they abandoned themselves to the joyous sense of intoxication which only wine could inspire, which made them feel *entheos*, one with the god, and to which, to the sixth century poet Theognis' sorrow, death put an end. Later they escorted the god's image on a ship-shaped waggon, to remind them not only of the traditional method of his advent, but of the resumption of navigation (as Nilsson suggested, and which has received unexpected support from a Linear B inscription), to the Ox-stall where the King Archon's wife sealed the bond between the people and their god in a primitive ritual marriage.

The only other Attic festival that was directly connected with

Dionysus as a wine-god was the somewhat mysterious Theoinia. It appears, to judge from the rather confused evidence, to have been essentially an ancestral festival, whose celebration was restricted to certain privileged demes or families. These were the ones originally associated with the vine's first introduction, and included the Koironidai, the Krokonidai and the Semachidai, as well as the Ikarieis, who had special connections with the drama. The feast was consequently celebrated only by the *gennetai*, that is to say members of the demes or families who claimed the privilege by ancestral right and not, as in the case of the Rural Dionysia, by all the demes. We are also told that the fourteen *Gerairai*, who assisted the Basilinna during the Anthesteria, acted as priestesses at the Theoinia and the later Iobaccheia. Of the details of the festival we are not informed, though we may infer that as it was connected with wine it may have had some features in common with the Anthesteria whose priestesses it shared. Its privileged ancestral character suggests that it was celebrated in early times, and almost certainly before the sixth century B.C.

That the Greeks did not regard Dionysus as a god of wine to the exclusion of everything else seems clear from the epithets applied to him. These include 'Within the Tree', 'Bough-Bearer', 'Bark', 'Ivy' and 'Flowery', as well as the more typical 'Of the sour grape', 'Bearer of Neat Wine', 'Rich in Grapes', 'Of the Wine-Press' and 'Smeared in Lees'. At the same time it were idle to deny that the association between the god and the vine was not always very close. The difficulty has always been to determine the precise relationship between the two. Otto, influenced largely by modern associations, maintained that wine was regarded by the Ancients as actually embodying the spirit of ecstasy typified by the god himself. Nilsson, on the other hand, regarded it as only an aid to enthusiasm which had come into Dionysus' province because the vine is a plant. Nilsson, in other words, as against Otto, denies that there was any connection between the vine and the orgiastic side of the Dionysiac religion, and his view gains support from Pindar and Plutarch. In fact it is hard to distinguish the daemon of frenzy from the god of vegetation, if indeed they are strictly separable at all. There was, as Farnell sagely remarked, only one Dionysus, though he was naturally viewed from different angles, and wine represented 'the quintessence of that god-life that moved in the juices and the sap of the earth'.

More interesting from the point of view that it recalled, however vaguely, the ecstatic side of Dionysiac worship was the Lenaia, a festival clearly distinct from the Anthesteria, though attempts have been made to equate the two. It was celebrated at the Lenaion, an Athenian shrine whose precise location has not yet been settled. Both the scholiast on Aristophanes' *Acharnians* and Stephanus of Byzantium, quoting Apollodorus, claim that it lay 'in the country'. But, as Deubner pointed out, there was probably some confusion with the Rural Dionysia, a mock celebration of which is included in the play. The ancient commentator on the passage in the famous speech on the Crown where Demosthenes accuses his rival Aeschines' mother of misbehaviour in the *kleision* near the shrine of the hero Calamites, states that this 'shed' adjoined the Lenaion and was situated in the Agora. Plato again refers to a part of the Agora as the 'orchestra', and Photius states quite definitely that Dionysiac contests were performed there and watched by spectators seated on *ikria*—wooden stands—in the days before the building of the Dionysiac theatre. This statement is not only of great interest in the history of the drama, but suggests that the earliest contests were associated with the Lenaion prior to the introduction of the cult of Dionysus Eleuthereus at Athens. In other words, at the beginning of the sixth century B.C. the worship of Dionysus was confined in Athens to the Lenaion in the Agora and to the shrine 'in the Marshes'.

The derivation of 'Lenaion' has been long debated, but there seems no doubt that any possible connection with *lenos*, a wine-press, can be denied on philological grounds. More likely it is connected with *lenai*, a title of the Bacchanals, which survives in the verb *lenaizousin* employed by Heraclitus as the equivalent of *bakcheuousin*. According to Professor Dodds the latter word meant to have a sense of communion with god, and not to rave, though it seems hard to deny that the outward manifestation of this sense was frenzy. There is, however, little evidence that scenes of Dionysiac abandon were enacted even in sober ritual form in archaic Athens. The paintings of Maenads pouring wine in the god's honour on a series of fifth century Attic stamnoi are not necessarily referable to any specific festival. The god's image in the vases consists of a mask and cloak, suspended on a pole. The practice of representing Dionysus by a mask was commemorated, during the sixth century, by the story that such a mask was mistaken for the countenance of the tyrant Pisistratus. The Lenaion, however, was not associated with wine, and if the paintings refer to any festival at all it must be the Anthesteria.

The inclusion of satyrs in some of the scenes and the imaginary names given to some of the women militate also against Pickard-Cambridge's cautious support for the view that the paintings referred to the Lenaia. For decorous and controlled figures are characteristic of the best fifth century art and are not necessarily reliable evidence for contemporary religion. An ancient commentator on Aristophanes' *Frogs* states that during the celebration of the Lenaia the *dadouchos* held a torch when pronouncing the formula 'Invoke the god!' to which the audience replied: 'Iacchus, son of Semele, giver of wealth——' This suggests that the main celebrations were held at night, but the mention of the *dadouchos* and Iacchus are proof of the gradual accretion of Eleusinian elements which would hardly have been present during the era with which we are concerned. Indeed the mutual borrowings between the Eleusinian Mysteries and the various Dionysiac festivals only became notable at the end of the sixth century B.C. Possibly some common elements rendered assimilation easier, though in the case of the Lenaia this cannot be proved.

A further argument against the Lenaia having been a wine festival is the season of its celebration. This was the month of Gamelion in Attica, which was roughly equivalent to January/February. The weather was then at its very unkindest, when the days were cold enough, in Hesiod's view, to flay an ox. Farnell thought the Lenaia was intended to rouse the slumbering deity, but his view was discredited by Pickard-Cambridge on the grounds of lack of evidence apart from what may be surmised by the free application of the comparative method. On the other hand the association of the Lenaion with a primitive *orchestra* suggests that dancing constituted an integral part of the celebrations, and this may have been performed by women dressed as Maenads.

The probability that Dionysus of the Lenaia reached Athens from Thebes is partially confirmed by the invocation to Iacchus as the son of Semele, who is described as a daughter of Cadmus even in Homer. What light the recent discovery of Babylonian inscriptions in the Cadmeia at Thebes may throw on Cadmus' eastern origins is not yet known, but the Lenaea, at any rate, seems to have been connected with the overland Thracian tradition and not with the cult that came over the sea.

The precise nature of the Lenaea depends largely on surmise. Probably the mood of the celebrants differed from that of the citizens who flocked to the sanctuary of Dionysus in the Marshes to seek the god's approval when they broached their casks. Here was the sophisticated but lineal survival of the Bacchic religion whose wilder excesses were remembered, if no longer practised in Attica. Indeed it seems doubtful whether the Lenaea preserved less decorous features even at the beginning of our period, as they would never have been tolerated by Solon. If they survived at all they must have been confined to outlying districts or to Cithaeron's rocky heights. The sixth century B.C. witnessed, above all, the final stages of the welding of the more intractable elements of alien cults into the great civic religions of the classical period.

The Lenaea, like the Anthesteria, is said to have included a procession and 'abuse from waggons'. But the authorities may be confusing the details of the two festivals. With regard to the nature of the dramatic contests held in the Agora we have no information. Presumably they would have been of a crude and primitive type analogous to the performances at the Rural Dionysia. Both tragedies and comedies were put on at the Lenaia during the fifth century B.C., but the tragedians naturally preferred the bigger audiences of the City Dionysia. Dithyrambs too were performed during later times so that the contests were probably not confined to a single type of drama. With the growth of interest in the drama during the sixth century the performances were removed to the theatre of Dionysus.

The origins of Greek drama remain tantalizingly obscure. Nevertheless the existence of a fragmentary inscription dating from the fifth century B.C. dealing with the accounts of the treasury of Dionysus suggest that Ikaria, whatever the truth about Thespis, was, like Eleutherae, a place where a Dionysiac cult was established prior to its introduction at Athens. A similar tradition was associated with Acharnae, the deme of Aristophanes' play. We may conjecture that these rural cults of Dionysus included many features too crude and possibly unrestrained for Athenian taste during the archaic period, and it was only through the tyrants' influence that their ceremonials were admitted into the city. Meantime the citizens contented themselves with the Lenaia and ignored the cruder *komoi* or processions celebrated in the local country-districts or demes.

Among these latter was the festival known as the Rural Dionysia, which was celebrated during the month Poseideon, that is to say in December. It consisted, as we gather from Aristophanes' *Acharnians*, of the carrying of a phallos in honour of Phales, a personification of the phallos, who is described as 'Comrade of the Rout'. The procession was headed by the usual *kanephoros*, with a crowd of revellers following. Such celebrations were dismissed with contempt by Heraclitus, who refers scathingly to those who hold processions in honour of Dionysus and sing a hymn to genitals.

If they did not hold a procession and sing a hymn to genitals, it would be an outrageous performance. Hades and Dionysus, in whose honour they rage and celebrate the Bacchus rites, are one and the same.

In other words the celebrants excused their obscene rites on the grounds that they were therein honouring their god. The question at once arises as to how far, if at all, phallic rites constituted an original part of Dionysiac worship. The evidence from vase painting is negative. The god, though sometimes accompanied by ithyphallic satyrs, was never depicted as phallic himself. Indeed the conclusion seems inevitable that local phallic cults became attached to a worship with which they had originally nothing to do. If this were so the Rural Dionysia was only Dionysiac in name and not in origin. As Deubner said, 'The phallos is not a symbol of Dionysus, but of the ancient independent fertility deity whose cult was absorbed by Dionysus.' Once, however, the processions had become associated with Dionysus the phallos became his emblem and was worn by actors in comedy. It is hard to trace the stages by which this transference occurred unless it was simply that the celebrants of the phallic processions lacked a deity, apart from the personified Phales, and were anxious to bring them into the sphere of the new and powerful god.

That the Rural Dionysia were not exclusively concerned with phallic worship, but also with the presentation of dramatic performances of some kind or other, is clear from the remains of theatres at Thorikos and Rhamnous as well as Ikaria. The two latter date from late classical times, but the theatre at Thorikos may be as old as the middle of the sixth century B.C. The reason why Dionysus and not Apollo, or some other deity, came to be associated with the drama was probably fortuitous. During the sixth century B.C. a remarkable marriage took place between the Peloponnesian dithyramb and Attic dialogue. As the dithyrambic hymn was sung primarily, if not exclusively, in honour of Dionysus, the drama which developed out of its conflation with dialogue was naturally included in the same god's sphere.

The original dithyramb, to judge from a fragment of Archilochus, was suitable for singing in a revel context. Presumably it included the element of wild abandon associated with Dionysiac *enthousiasmos*. Later Arion of Methymna produced a new literary form of the dithyramb to be sung by a trained chorus. The chorus was not a wandering one, but remained in one place, and sang separate themes concerned presumably with the adventures of Dionysus, under separate titles. In this innovation we may already sense a sufficient element of drama to have rendered the later conflation with dialogue both natural and easy, though Koller has recently suggested that the dramatic form of the dithyramb was novel.

During the sixth century B.C. Lasos introduced dithyrambic contests at Athens, which were doubtless also performed in the demes. Indeed the theatre at Thorikos may have witnessed such performances prior to the invention of the drama as such. The performances were fostered presumably by the tyrants who were also probably instrumental in popularizing, if not in actually founding, the Great or City Dionysia. Peasant gods in fact became popular, as Burn observed, when peasants came into the city.

This famous festival, which was second only in importance to the Panathenaea, was held in honour of Dionysus Eleuthereus whose cult was said to have been introduced at Athens at some time undefined by a certain Pegasos. The men of Athens, like Lycurgus and Pentheus in myth, were said at first to have resisted the new worship and neglected to honour the deity. As a result the god punished them with impotence. When they applied to the Delphic oracle for aid they were told to make model phalloi. In the circumstances the oracle's advice was appropriate, and need not be interpreted as indicating that the cult possessed phallic features.

Whatever the real date of the cult's introduction (and there is at least a possibility that it was associated with the voluntary transference of Eleutherae from the Theban to the Athenian alliance), we are told that the old wooden image was conveyed from the local temple to Athens where it was presumably housed in the older Pisistratid temple.

It may be surmised that the cult made no immediate impression in Athens, and that it was not until the onset of the plague, coupled with the oracle's advice, that the citizens' attention was drawn to their culpable neglect. This may have been the very opportunity that Pisistratus was seeking, and he founded the new festival for its popular appeal. That the institution was late is virtually proved by its having been placed under the control of the Eponymous Archon, and not that of the King Archon himself. For the rest we are left to conjecture from the evidence the probable course of events.

The original aim of the City Dionysia was, presumably, to placate Dionysus Eleuthereus for his mean reception in the city. Hence it commenced with a ritual repetition of the god's original arrival, except that he was now welcomed with special honours. His image was escorted in daylight to an altar in the Academy, which lay on the road to Eleutherae, and after the offering of a sacrifice and the singing of hymns it was escorted back by torchlight to the theatre where it presided over the dramatic contests. The chief actors in the ritual procession were the ephebes. Possibly they were given the rôle by Pisistratus who would have been naturally anxious to curry favour with the warrior youth. The final procession, which probably took place on the following morning, was headed by a *kanephoros* and included a bull, escorted by the ephebes, as well as the bearers of bloodless sacrifices. Most striking of all were the red-robed Metics and the splendidly attired choregoi, who produced the plays.

Phalloi, we are told, were carried in the procession, though this might well have been expected having regard to the manner in which the god was originally placated. Probably too there was much singing and abuse in the light-hearted manner of all popular feasts. After the procession the day was occupied with dithyrambic contests and closed, apparently, with a revel. Probably all the features so far enumerated formed part of the original festival at the time of its founding and/or development by Pisistratus. A number of circumstances insured the popularity and growth of the City Dionysia. First and foremost the propaganda possibilities of the dramatic contests whose formal development did not so much coincide with as constitute a basic element in its foundation. Second the universal appeal of a spring festival, for the City Dionysia was held during the month of Elaphebolion—March—when the weather had grown warmer, and visitors could travel safely by sea. Soon the brilliance of the dramatic presentations outshone the other religious features to the virtual exclusion of Dionysus himself. Only the humble Anthesteria preserved the tradition of the Thraco-Phrygian deity who had introduced the vine to Attica. Of his wilder orgies and the savage omophagy, the eating of raw flesh, practised by his thyrsos-armed devotees, nothing survived except vestigially in the Lenaia, and in the rites of the Thyiads who revelled on Parnassus in honour, it was said, of Apollo and Dionysus together.

Heraclitus stated in the fragment already quoted that 'Hades and Dionysus are one and the same, in whose honour the Bacchanals rage and rave', and indeed the existence of residual chthonian features in the worship of Dionysus, despite their virtual absence in the state cults, is only to be expected. The Thraco-Phrygian region was notable not only for ecstatic forms of religion but also for a curious belief in an immortality transcending earthly life. 'The belief of the Getae where immortality is concerned,' says Herodotus, 'is as follows. They believe that they don't really die, but that when they forsake this life they go to Zalmoxis.' Later the historian contrasts the lamentation which greets a child's birth among the Trausi, a Thracian tribe, with the joy displayed at a man's funeral. Again, the Thracian king Rhesus, like Amphiaraus, possessed chthonian powers, and lived in a cave on Mount Pangaion in the capacity of a demi-god. Traces of most of these beliefs survive in the Dionysiac religion. First and foremost Dionysus was associated with a form of ecstatic possession which conferred on its votaries a sense of vicarious immortality. Secondly he promoted fertility, though not because his mother was an earth deity, for her equation with the Zemelo of the Phrygian inscription, who appeared to be the counterpart of Zeus, has been discredited. Again visitors to his oracle at Amphikleia practised incubation, a rite peculiarly associated with chthonian powers. Finally the strange legend of the duel between Xanthus, the Boeotian, and the Neleid Melanthus in which the latter gained the victory through the opportune epiphany of Dionysus Melanaigis, i.e. of the Black Goatskin, reads like a ritual description of the seasonal victory of winter over summer, as Usener first saw. That the drama had some basis in such ritual mummery seems likely, and gains support from the other story told about Dionysus Melanaigis. According to this the daughters of Eleuther, the eponymous hero of Eleutherae, the frontier village from which the cult of Dionysus Eleuthereus came to Athens, once reviled an epiphany of Dionysos Melanaigis and were driven mad in consequence.

In conclusion it must be confessed that in tracing the history of the Dionysiac religion the scholar is continually faced with a curious contradiction. The tradition that Dionysus was one of the younger gods dies hard. Indeed some of his associations appear very old. In Lesbos, where Zeus, Hera and Dionysus constituted an unusual triad, an explanation has been sought in the possibility that his worship on the island antedated that of the two Olympians. His subsequent admission to Olympus at Hera's instance need not necessarily prove that his worship was newer than that of the other gods, but merely of an alien nature. At Methymna, again, he was represented as a primitive wooden idol, while his temple at Breia, like that at Athens 'in the Marshes', was regarded as exceedingly old. In fact one is sometimes forced to the conclusion that the Dionysiac cult was not so much a novelty as a revival of something far older, analogous even to the ancient Cretan religion with its ecstatic features, nature worship and strange bull ritual. Likelihood is lent to this possibility by the occurrence, already noted, of the god's name in two Linear B inscriptions, association with the mysterious Zagreus, who will be discussed later in connection with Orpheus, and the legend of Ariadne's abandonment by Theseus on the island of Naxos and subsequent marriage to Dionysus.

But it is with the revival, not the origin, of the Dionysiac religion that we have been mainly concerned here, and with its gradual acceptance among the official state cults. The final stages of this process took place during the sixth century B.C. and culminated in the god's admission to Delphi. His tomb there, as at Thebes, perpetuated the strange legend of his dismemberment by the Titans, and upon this and the Cretan myth of Zagreus the Orphics appear to have based their way of life.

DIONYSUS

No mention has been made here of Satyrs and Silens, though the latter first appear in association with Dionysus in mid-sixth century art. The alliance was a natural one as the fertility spirits of nature had much in common with the deity who gave life to trees and plants. That the caprine and equine daemons of Greek imagination had no place in serious religion it would be rash to deny. Certainly they had some place in cult if Professor Webster is right in identifying the dramatic participants in the phallic procession as disguised satyrs. The theory is supported by the representation of grotesque and padded figures in association with phalloi on black-figured ware. The drunken Silens were not sharply differentiated from the Satyrs much before the sixth century B.C., though they were credited with supernatural wisdom and were consequently revered. Indeed there is a moving dignity about the Silen carved during the sixth century B.C. on one of the gates of Thasos that is far removed from *Satyrspiele*. Both Satyrs and Silens belong, like the Sphinxes and Sirens, to the fascinating borderland between religion and mythology where definitions of both become blurred. But it is time to consider the Orphic religion whose powerful impact affected, in some degree, almost all subsequent western religious life.

NOTES TO CHAPTER IV

Page 78. Ionia. Cf. Herodotus, I, 150; Dodds, *Bacchae*[2], p. xxi; *IG*, II[2], 1368.

79. Older Dionysia. Cf. Thucydides, II, 15.

Anthesteria. Cf. Farnell, *CGS*, v, pp. 221 ff.; Pickard-Cambridge, *DF*, p. 9; Palmer, *The Interpretation of Mycenaean Greek Texts*, p. 255.

Choes. Cf. Farnell, op. cit., p. 319 n., 124K.

80. Sacred Marriage. Cf. Pickard-Cambridge, *DF*, p. 11.

Bull. Cf. Iliad, VI, 130 f.; Aeschylus, *fgm.* 54; Farnell, op. cit., pp. 126 ff., 217; Dodds, op. cit., p. xxvii, n. 1.

Abuse from the waggons. Cf. Farnell, op. cit., pp. 211–12; Pickard-Cambridge, op. cit., p. 12.

Chytroi. Cf. Farnell, op. cit., pp. 317 ff. and refs.; Pickard-Cambridge, op. cit., p. 4; Snodgrass, *JHS*, 1964, p. 116.

81. Comic agones. Cf. Plutarch, *Dec. Orat. Vit.*, 7, 1, 10.

Theatre. Cf. Pickard-Cambridge, *Theatre*, pp. 3 ff.

Intoxication. Cf. Theognis, 976; Dodds, op. cit., p. xiii.

Navigation. Cf. Nilsson, *Geschichte*[2], 1, 550; Palmer, op. cit., p. 254.

82. Theoinia. Cf. Farnell, op. cit., pp. 206 ff., 314 and notes.

    God of moisture. Cf. Pindar, *fgm.* 153; Plutarch, 356A; Farnell, op. cit., p. 122; Otto, *Dionysos*, p. 135; Nilsson, op. cit., p. 585.

83. Lenaea. Cf. Pickard-Cambridge, *DF*, pp. 36 ff (Apol. 26 E).

    Lenaion. Cf. Farnell, op. cit., p. 208; Deubner, op. cit., p. 124; Pickard-Cambridge, *DF*, 32 ff.; Dodds, op. cit., p. xii.

    Vases. Cf. Deubner, op. cit., pp. 126 ff.; Pickard-Cambridge, op. cit., p. 27.

    Pisistratus. Cf. Athenaeus, 533C.

84. Gamelion. Cf. Hesiod, *W&D*, 504.

    Cadmus. Cf. Iliad, XIV, 323 f.; Hawkes, 'Linear B at Thebes', *Observer*, July 5, 1964.

85. Cithaeron. Cf. Dodds, op. cit., p. XXXI, n. 1.

    Attic cults. Cf. Deubner, op. cit., p. 136, n. 2; Pickard-Cambridge, op. cit., pp. 39, 45; *DTC*², p. 72, no. 1.

86. Rural Dionysia. Cf. Heraclitus, *fgm.* 127 (Bywater); Aristophanes, *Acharnians*, 202, 241 f.; Farnell, op. cit., pp. 313 n., 106A.

87. Dithyramb. Cf. Pickard-Cambridge, op. cit., pp. 19 ff.; Koller, 'Dithyrambos und Tragödie', *Glotta*, 1962, pp. 183 ff.

    Dionysia. Cf. Farnell, op. cit., p. 230; Pickard-Cambridge, *DF*, pp. 56 ff.; Burn, *The Lyric Age of Greece*, p. 346.

    Lycurgus and Pentheus. Cf. Homer, *Iliad*, VI, 130 ff.; Dodds, op. cit. pp. xxv ff. and 144.

89. Omophagy. Cf. Dodds, op. cit., pp. xvi f.

    Getae. Cf. Herodotus, IV, 94; Metzger, 'Dionysos Chthonien', *JDAI*, LXVIII, 1953, pp. 39 ff.

    Trausi. Cf. Herodotus, V, 4.

    Rhesus. Cf. Dodds, op. cit., p. xxvii, n. 1.

    Semele. Cf. Dodds, op. cit., p. 63, n. 3.

    Xanthus and Melanthus. Cf. Scholia to Aristophanes, *Acharnians*, 146, and Plato, *Symposium*, 208D; Usener, *Archiv für Religionswissenschaft*, 1904, pp. 303–13.

90. Melanaigis. Cf. Pausanias, II, 35, 1; Scholiast to Aristophanes, *Acharnians*, 146.

    Lesbos. Cf. Page, *Sappho and Alcaeus*, pp. 168 ff. For Keos of Caskey, *Hesperia*, 1964.

    Zagreus. Cf. Dodds, op. cit., p. xxi, no. 3.

    Satyrs. Cf. Pickard-Cambridge, *DTC*², pp. 118 ff.; Brommer, *Satyroi*; Webster, *Greek Art and Literature, 700–530 B.C.*, pp. 60 ff; Patzer, *Die Anfänge der griechischen Tragödie*, 1962; Picard, *Thasos*, 1962. For Parthenos at Neopolis of Lazarides, *A Delt.* 17, 235 f.

CHAPTER V

THE FOLLOWERS OF ORPHEUS

There is a natural tendency among scholars, influenced doubtless by the archaic nature of the monuments and the comparative dearth of literary remains, to regard the sixth century B.C. as in some ways a primitive era. If there be truth in this view at all it is only in the sense that the more primitive elements were more primitive still, for though the flowering time of the Greek genius was concentrated mainly in the two following centuries the seeds of its great achievements were sown during the previous hundred years. Philosophy and the drama, as we know it, both first appeared during this major period of development, while art achieved its canonical form. Lyric poetry again was at its most brilliant best, while the support given to religious observances by the Tyrants for political motives deepened the interest in religion itself. For in addition to the growing popularity of religious festivals and the raising of splendid temples in honour of the gods there was a general craving for something more intimate, personal and satisfying than had ever been provided by the city cults. It was all very well to pray to Dionysus for the prosperity of the grape-harvest or to Athena to preserve the state in war, but these were matters of general importance which did not affect the individual life. The myths of Homer and Hesiod had sufficed for a previous age when it came to matters of teleology. But now men were beginning to seek a more direct approach to the gods, and a more definite assurance upon such age-old problems as the possibility of life after death. So while the state cults prospered the appeal of the new mystery religions grew stronger still, and there were not wanting sages, seers and prophets who were either credited with supernatural wisdom or claimed direct contact with a god. Most famous and influential of these was the Delphic Pythia, but the less authentic prophecies of Bacis and Sibylla were also commonly believed. There were, in addition, certain religious innovators who founded a way of life. Notable among these were the Orphics and Pythagoreans, both of whom were destined to have a profound effect on subsequent religious thought. Unfortunately our knowledge of both during the sixth century B.C. is so shadowy as to be, in the case of the Orphics, virtually non-existent. Indeed even our one piece of firm evidence has been attacked by Linforth. According to Pausanias, Onomacritus, the unscrupulous editor who was exiled by the tyrant Hipparchus for inserting forged oracles into the canon of Musaeus, first devised 'orgia', that is to say 'holy rites', for Dionysus, and made the Titans the authors of his sufferings. Now although Pausanias does not mention Orpheus in this connection, the legend of the dismemberment of Dionysus was mentioned in Orphic poems according to Diodorus, who flourished during the first century B.C., by Tatian in Pausanias' own day and later by Clement of Alexandria, Philoponus, Sextus Empiricus and the Souda, a Byzantine lexicon of the tenth century A.D., formerly known as Suidas. Linforth, however, considered that Pausanias' statement was entirely speculative and had no basis in historical fact. Yet Herodotus' evidence that Onomacritus was responsible for interpolations in Musaeus, coupled with the tradition preserved by the Byzantine scholar Tsetzes that he was a member of the board appointed by Pisistratus to edit Homer, lends at least some degree of likelihood to Pausanias' views. In both literature and art Orpheus was a familiar figure in the sixth century B.C. He is termed 'Orpheus of famous name', by Ibycus, though we do not know the context, and is included with the Argonauts under the title of 'Orphas' in an early sixth century Delphic relief, which has been thought to derive from the Syracusan Treasury. Orpheus was taken by Jason, according to the historian Herodorus, on the advice of the wise Centaur Chiron, in order to help the heroes pass the Sirens, who duly plunged into the sea when his music surpassed their own. He was supposed, like Dionysus, to have come from Thrace, though he was distinguished by dress from the Thracians in vase representations, possibly, as Guthrie suggests, to emphasize his missionary capacity. Euripides, on the other hand, associates him with Olympus, a tradition in keeping with the legend that the Muse Calliope was his mother. His father was the Thracian river-god Oeagrus, though Apollo was also sometimes said to have been his sire. Like Musaeus, Homer and Hesiod, he was commonly regarded as primarily a teacher, though his medium of instruction was the lyre. He was said by Aeschylus in Aristophanes' *Frogs* to have introduced rites of initiation, and taught men to refrain from bloodshed. Protagoras too defends the art of sophistic on the grounds that famous poets like Homer, Hesiod and Simonides practised it overtly, as did the followers of Orpheus and Musaeus. The author again of the pseudo-Euripidean Rhesus states that Orpheus 'introduced the torches of the secret mysteries', where the reference is presumably to Athens.

There is no evidence that the Orphics formed a sect, at any rate in the early period, as has sometimes been supposed. They were individual adepts, and represented, as H. J. Rose observed in his review of Linforth's work, 'an attitude not a cult, still less at that date, a body of dogma'. The authority to which they turned, and upon which they apparently based their observances, were the poems which existed under the name of Orpheus, and which are referred to alongside those of Homer, Hesiod and Musaeus by Aristophanes, the author of the speech against Aristogeiton, Euripides, Plato, Hippias and Alexis. In later times there existed a considerable corpus of Orphic poems, but little that may be referred with certainty to the archaic era, but the habit of making Musaeus his mouthpiece suggested to Linforth that even in early times Orpheus was regarded rather as the source of inspiration than as the actual composer of the poems.

'I have found nought stronger than Fate,' sings the chorus in Euripides' *Alcestis*, 'not even a charm on the Thracian tablets which Orpheus' voice inscribed.' In other words the great musician's precepts were recorded by poets on tablets, and were familiar to everyone in Athens in the tragedian's day. Such, at least, is Linforth's interpretation of a passage which it is difficult to explain satisfactorily in other ways. It is true that the ancient commentator states that Heraclides of Pontus, a contemporary of Plato, claimed that records, inscribed on tablets, existed in his day on Mount Haemus in Thrace, at a shrine of or in honour of Dionysus. But there was no necessary connection with Orpheus.

It has, of course, been not infrequently assumed that the sayings of Orpheus preserved in the poems inspired certain enlightened spirits to react, in the archaic period, against the barbarity of the Dionysiac omophagia. Certainly the legend of Orpheus' dismemberment by the Bassarides, the Bacchantes of Thrace, suggests the existence of some traditional enmity between the singer and the god. But to argue from this that the followers of Orpheus took it upon themselves to attempt to reform the Dionysiac revelry in the light of their own beliefs is to go much further than the evidence will allow. Indeed we do not know that the early Orphics were reformers at all in the formal sense, only that their asceticism was opposed to the normal way of life and sometimes excited criticism.

That Orpheus was in some way associated with Apollo there is good reason to believe. Pindar, at any rate, says so, though the precise relationship he leaves in doubt, and the mood of the Orphics themselves with their emphasis on purity and restraint has outwardly more in common with Delphi than with the wild cults of Thrace. At all times the Orphics stood apart from the general masses by their insistence on following a rigid code of living, which was perhaps characterized by some degree of arrogance, if the fate of their founder be anything to go on. But this is never emphasized in the authorities, though they were naturally open to the charge of being quacks or prigs. Their attitude to their fellow men is perhaps best exemplified by the familiar hexameter quoted by Plato, 'Many bear the wand [of Dionysus], but few are true adepts', though whether he had the Orphics in mind is not quite certain.

The canons laid down for the Orphics to follow were all of a simple and practical nature, if directed in the main to the ascetically inclined. First and foremost they precluded meat eating, and the spreading of pollution through the medium of animal skins.

'No woollen articles are carried into their temples,' says Herodotus of the Egyptians, 'or buried with them. For it is contrary to their religion. In this way they resemble the so-called Orphics and Pythagoreans.'

Aristophanes' reference to Orphic abstention from slaughter has already been mentioned, while Plato writes of the sacred books of Musaeus and Orpheus, 'in accordance with which they offer sacrifice'.

'Clothed in white I avoid men's births, touch not the coffins of the dead, and refrain from eating the flesh of living creatures,' sang Euripides' chorus in the Cretans. Finally Plato summarizes the contemporary view about Orphic practices in a notable passage in the Laws.

'They refrained from meat because they considered that it was sacrilegious either to eat it or to pollute the gods' altars with blood; and so there arose among our forebears the kind of life that is called Orphic, and which retains everything that is lifeless and abstains from everything that lives————'

The striking point about all these passages is that with the specific exception of flesh-eating they are mainly concerned with popular tabus. The avoidance of physical pollution by death was by no means only confined to Orphics, but was practised by the followers of Pythagoras, and the purging of defilement occasioned by bloodshed much exercised the Delphic oracle during the archaic period as we have seen. Such purging may have had repercussions in the non-human sphere, and could even have occasioned the tabu on meat. If it was wrong for men to slay one another, it was equally wrong to kill other living things. Again the primeval tabu against cannibalism could be logically extended to beasts. During the sixth century B.C. men seem to have pondered these questions more deeply than in previous eras, and worked out for themselves their religious implications. Belief in transmigration of the soul, which is widespread even to this day in Tibet, was by no means a novel phenomenon. All children are animists and Pythagoreans at heart and most men share this consciousness in varying degrees. The Orphics took advantage of ancient tabus, and included them in their canon. Hence the problem of separating Orphic elements from Pythagorean may not be a real one. Pherecydes, we are told, made a collection of Orphic sayings during the fifth century B.C., but the poems were regarded as being at least coeval with those of Homer and Hesiod and were doubtless written down much earlier. On them was based a way of life which appealed to men of nobler instincts, and rites were instituted in honour of the supposed originator of the sayings.

That the founder of a lofty way of life should be credited with magical powers in an era of magicians and miracle-workers is hardly surprising, but by the fifth century they had become a suitable subject for a satyr play.

'I am acquainted with a fine spell of Orpheus,' says the chorus in the Cyclops, 'which will cause the brand to advance of its own accord to burn the one-eyed child of earth.' The reference, of course, is to the parody of the Homeric Polyphemus episode, which the satyrs are busy enacting on the stage. A charm, again, is mentioned in connection with the passage in the *Alcestis* which has already been discussed. The tendency to include Orphics in the same class as oracle-mongers and other impostors in the fifth and subsequent centuries B.C. was a natural consequence of the spread of rationalism combined with political and moral decline. According to Plutarch, king Leotychidas of Sparta was once visited by an Orphic quack called Philip, who lived in great poverty. When he informed the king that those who were initiated found happiness after death, the king rejoined, 'Why then don't you drop dead and end your misery?' Nonconformity, whether in the political or in the religious sphere, is always open to attack, and the unpopularity of the Orphics with ordinary orthodox citizens is well illustrated by Theseus' bitter comments on what he wrongly regarded as the hypocrisy of Hippolytus' ascetic form of life. Plutarch's sneer that the Orphic heaven consisted of endless drunkenness was an attack in the same vein.

It was shown in the last chapter that very little survived in the state cults of the wilder elements of the Dionysiac religion. For its roots we have to go much further back than the sixth century B.C. So with the Orphics. The association of Eurydice with Orpheus, whether an original feature of the myth, or, as Guthrie supposed, an attachment from some other source, suggests that, like Dionysus, he acquired chthonian overtones in Thrace. The story of his going to fetch his wife from the underworld was known to Euripides, where his quest was successful, and to Plato who said he was beguiled with a phantom, as well as to Isocrates who also credits him with having brought the dead back from Hades. Her absence in Polygnotus' painting is undoubtedly due to the fact, as Linforth indicated, that his descent into the underworld could not have been made contemporaneous with Odysseus' later visit. Sacramental features were certainly emphasized in later times when the dead were furnished with detailed guides, as in the gold plates discovered in Crete and Italy. Indeed the Orphics held no monopoly where the underworld was concerned. Though largely in abeyance after the Persian wars the widespread popularity of mystery cults during the previous era bears ample witness to a general concern with the highly personal problem of survival. Doubtless the Pisistratids at Athens encouraged this tendency for their own purposes. The Orphics certainly seem to have been much exercised to find a solution through the observance of a way of life based on asceticism. This, to judge from the list of tabus, was far more concerned with the everyday morality of the ordinary citizen than were, for example, the Eleusinian Mysteries. The latter provided a great psychic experience on a unique occasion, but did not lay down in detail the rules by which the Initiates should live. By promulgating the doctrine of 'Soma sema—the body is a tomb', the Orphics were ultimately responsible for Platonism and the dualism which continued henceforward to haunt all Greek thought. The doctrine was not, of course, a new one. The elaborate Egyptian concern with the other world was well known to the Greeks, as well as the monstrous conceptions of the adjacent Orient. But the aristocratic world of Homer, whose views had predominated at Athens, passed away during the sixth century B.C. and ordinary man found less to comfort him than had the rich landowners of former times. Unlike Achilles he was only too willing to believe that there were better things in store for the underprivileged in the world to come, and that it was important to lead a good life to attain this desirable end.

The germ of the soma-sema doctrine has been found in the legend of the slaying and devouring of Dionysus by the Titans, from whose ashes men were created. This has been interpreted as implying that everyone's Titanic nature contains a spark of the divine in it. Despite Pausanias' statement that Onomacritus was ultimately responsible for introducing this legend into the Dionysiac myth it seems hardly possible that such an arresting feature could have been invented or manipulated by one man, particularly as he was living at the very time when the Orphics were developing their way of life. Perhaps Onomacritus gave prominence to a feature which surely must have existed in some form previously. New myths were not created suddenly, as Marót has recently emphasized, or new twists given to old tales by such conservative minded people as the Greeks. The essence of the story of the cannibalistic feast must, like so much else concerned with Dionysus and Orpheus, have originated in Thrace, though Guthrie disagrees. The interesting series of gold plates found in graves in Crete and south Italy, some of which may date from the fourth century B.C., has been accepted as Orphic by many scholars, mainly on the grounds of subject matter which is largely concerned with heavenly lineage and purification from sin, all of which seems to accord well with the Titan myth. But though Persephone and other deities are mentioned, Orpheus never is.

To the ordinary man who wondered why he had not been born rich or privileged or healthy or strong the Orphic priests explained that punishments in this life were awarded for transgressions in a previous one. That they were in fact the originators of this doctrine, which bears a striking resemblance to Buddhist belief, is shown by Plato who says in the *Cratylus*: 'I think the disciples of Orpheus are in the main responsible for giving it the designation [sema-tomb], believing as they do that the soul is being punished for some reason or other, and has this husk about it, like a prison, to prevent it from running away——', though Pindar is the first literary authority to explain the immortality of the soul by its heavenly origin.

That such an eschatological view was readily open to abuse is clear from Plato's criticism of the performance by the Orphics of 'teletai-rites', which permitted men to obtain redemption from their transgressions. But in the sixth century when the advocates of Orphism were making their way the element of corruption was probably not emphatic. Men were avid to learn a way of life which culminated in personal salvation. Yet the canon of Orphism was too harsh for the majority and it was not until the succeeding century that loop-holes were detected and taken advantage of by less serious devotees. Then the spells mentioned in the Cyclops doubtless came into their own, and the patent dishonesty of charlatan priests shocked honest men.

The familiar underworld torments of burial in mud or filth, and filling leaky pitchers, were included in Orphic eschatology, and clearly formed part of popular myth. That of the leaky pitchers constituted the particular punishment of the uninitiated, and was an appropriate enough fate for non-Orphics too. The allegorical associations of burial in mud are discussed by Guthrie. Indeed its moral is so obvious that it is reasonable to suppose that it constituted an original feature of Orphic dogma. As for the cycle of reincarnation it too was bound up with the myth of the Titans. Pindar, quoted by Socrates in the Meno, says '[To those] from whom Persephone accepts atonement for ancient grief, in the ninth year she restores their souls again to the sun above'. This passage was analysed by H. J. Rose.

The fragment, on internal grounds, may be early, and written possibly only a decade after the close of the sixth century itself. Hence anything which it may reveal of Orphic doctrine is highly relevant to its formative period. 'Penthos' must mean 'grief', as the word is mainly employed in this subjective sense both in Homer and in Pindar. The 'grief' again for which Persephone accepts atonement must be her own. Again, as mortals were not concerned in her rape, the 'grief' which the poet refers to could only have been occasioned by the loss of her son at the hands of the Titans, from whose ashes the human race was reputed to have sprung. Persephone's son was the mysterious Zagreus, who was apparently stated by Aeschylus to have been a son of Hades. He is usually associated with Crete in legend, but may well have been in origin a chthonian god from Thrace. He was at any rate identified with Cretan Zeus and also with Dionysus. In return for their sin of being descended from the Titans the angry goddess demanded the full eight years' term of penance, at least in Boeotia, from those guilty of bloodshed. Manifestly only a chosen few succeeded in satisfying Persephone's terms and these became men of influence. The general run of mankind suffered a lengthier period of purgatory. As Persephone is omitted from the parallel passages quotable from Pindar which are concerned with eschatology, the probability that this passage refers specifically to the Orphics is considerably heightened.

In the Meno Socrates mentions the authority of 'men and women who were wise in sacred lore' in connection with the doctrine of the immortality of the soul. He defines them furthermore as 'holy men and women of the type who make it their business to be able to give an account of what they undertake to do——' This, as Guthrie notices, is a good description of the distinctive characteristics of the Orphics, and suggested to H. J. Rose that, at least by Pindar's time, they had acquired their own clergy. There was, on the other hand, no suggestion of an Orphic cult as such.

Not only did the Orphics construct an eschatology, but also an effective theogony, and presumably at an early date. Most of the evidence derives from the fragments of the Rhapsodic Theogony preserved by the Neoplatonists. The date of this work is examined by Guthrie, who, in the light of Gruppe's observations, succeeds in extracting certain ancient and basic doctrines out of it. First and foremost was the doctrine of the One, familiar as the dogma of the Ionian physicists. Oceanus again, the water principle, already familiar to Homer, was, in Plato's view, father of the Orphic deities. According, however, to the more usual account Time was first born from the primeval mud and, in turn, fashioned an egg in Aether, the element of Sky. From the egg sprang Phanes-Erikepaios, the primal god. He married Night and they begot Heaven and Earth. The rest agreed in the main with Hesiod, except that Zeus was said to have swallowed Phanes and created the universe anew, which in Guthrie's view might represent a conscious effort to supply a creator. Throughout Zeus seeks the counsel of Night, who is treated as a supreme deity even in the Iliad. The jealousy of the Titans resulted in the rending and tasting of Dionysus, who was nevertheless reborn. The monstrous description of Chronos or Time in the Hieronymian version suggests oriental influence even at an early stage. But this is hardly surprising. If the Greek imagination could be stimulated and influenced by oriental art during the archaic period there seems no reason why it should not have been similarly influenced by the symbolism which inspired it. Orphic literature at any rate seems to have revelled in the grimmer side of Greek mythology. The accurate details of the original Orphic theogony we shall, in all probability, never be privileged to know. Nevertheless the egg described in Aristophanes' parody has been generally regarded as an original Orphic feature. Again, according to the comic-poet, it was a 'wind-egg', that is one laid by a hen without recourse to a cock. In practice it would be sterile, and this is part of Aristophanes' joke, but it could also imply that it had been laid by Night, the primeval element, independently of a consort. The absence of any reference to Phanes before Diodorus (50 B.C.), who quotes an Orphic fragment linking his name with Dionysus, coupled with the primacy yielded to Night in Homer, suggests that Phanes was an interloper. Aristophanes, at any rate, says that Eros, Love, came out of the egg. Possibly Phanes was, as Gruppe suggested, of oriental origin, and became identified with Metis, Wisdom, whom Zeus also swallowed, and the mysterious Erikepaios. It would certainly have been in keeping with the tendency of the early Orphics to base their dogmas on accepted systems. As Night had achieved primacy or near-primacy in Homer and Hesiod they had no wish to displace her.

With regard to the relationship of the Orphics to Dionysus all views must be largely conjectural. The Cretan complication with the Zeus of Ida suggests that a form of ecstatic worship survived from the Minoan in historical times, and that when the worship of Dionysus was introduced, or indeed re-introduced, the two deities were naturally identified. But there is no evidence to show that the early Orphics were much concerned with the Cretan development. Their main concern was to achieve the goal of personal purity in accordance with the dictates of the Orphic canon as preserved in the poems. That this was in some sense a mystical and ritual process seems clear from the circumstance that Orpheus himself came to be regarded as the originator of the rites of religious initiation, and also as the author of mysteries. The possibility that the Apolline element in Orpheus was due to Delphic propaganda, as H. J. Rose suggested, cannot be gainsaid. During the sixth century B.C. the oracle's influence became powerful everywhere throughout the Greek world, and even beyond, as we have already seen. The tendency to explain everything that possibly could be so explained in terms of Apollo was an essential part of the Delphic creed. As the rival activities of Dionysus could not be so explained the new religion, after undergoing due katharsis, was introduced at Apolline headquarters. That the Orphics actively assisted in the Delphic attempt to rationalize and control the Dionysiac religion cannot of course be proved, or that they were openly in league with Delphi at any time. The suspicion, however, remains. The statement in pseudo-Eratosthenes that Dionysus was angry with Orpheus because he considered Helios-Apollo the greatest of the gods, and ascended mount Pangaion to greet the dawn, cannot be taken seriously for the earlier periods, as there is no evidence that Apollo was identified with the sun-god, even by poets, until the fifth century. There was, however, as has been mentioned in Chapter I, a tradition, preserved by Pausanias, that Orpheus visited Delphi when Thamyras, the Thracian poet, who competed with the Muses, and Philammon, the celebrated singer, entered the musical competition, but after talking solemnly of his rites disdained to take part. His ritual associations are also mentioned by the same author in connection with the family of the Lycomidae at Phyla, and with an oracle at Lesbos of dubious authenticity, while his statue was shown standing with that of Ritual personified on Helicon.

The resemblance between the lives led by the Orphics and the early Pythagoreans was noted in ancient times, and actually persuaded Wilamowitz that the system was Pythagorean. Herodotus, as we have seen, grouped the two together, while Ion of Chios, Euripides' contemporary, stated that Pythagoras had attributed his own poems to Orpheus. But the Orphics, unlike the Pythagoreans, laid claim only to a legendary founder and not to a historical personage. Neither did they seek to meddle in politics or to persuade the generality to adopt their views. All they did was to attempt to provide a religious explanation for the problems concerned with death and homicide which had worried the Greeks from Homer's day, but which achieved a far wider significance after the break-up of the clans. The notion of a brotherhood of sin, in which all men shared, must have appealed strongly to the new detribalized classes which appeared during the sixth century B.C. The Pythagoreans, meanwhile, were concerned with achieving the same kind of katharsis that the Orphics aimed at, only by another means. While practising abstinence from flesh-eating, over-indulgence in beans, and believing in the doctrine of transmigration, the cycle of birth, and the dualism of body and soul, they regarded the study of the science of mathematics as leading to ultimate salvation. Like those of the Ionian physicists both systems started from a single concept, which the Orphics called an egg and the Pythagoreans a monad. Both systems again admitted some degree of mysticism, though not in identical terms. Nevertheless the Pythagoreans' concern with the harmony of the universe brought them close to Orpheus with his harp. Both too were in some sense shamans and characteristic of their time and age.

NOTES TO CHAPTER V

Page 94. Orphics. Cf. Linforth, *The Arts of Orpheus*, pp. xvi ff., 214 ff. and 350 ff.

Dismemberment. Cf. Nilsson, 'Early Orphism and Kindred Religious Movements', *HThR*, XXVIII, 1935, pp. 195 ff.; Linforth, op. cit., pp. 350 ff.

Origins. Cf. Guthrie, *Orpheus*, p. 62, note to Chapter III; 1, p. 63.

95. Bloodshed. Cf. Aristophanes, *Frogs*, 1032–3; Plato, *Protagoras*, 316D. For Rhesus cf. Linforth, op. cit., pp. 61 ff; Ritchie, *Rhesus*.

Review of Linforth. Cf. *CR*, 1943, pp. 33–4.

Thracian tablets. Cf. Euripides, *Alcestis*, 968; Linforth, op. cit., pp. 120 ff.

96. Bassarides. Cf. Nilsson, loc. cit., pp. 203 ff.

Apollo. Cf. Pindar, *Pyth.*, IV, p. 178.

True adepts. Cf. Plato, *Phaedo*, 69C.

Woollen articles. Cf. Herodotus, II, 81; Linforth, op. cit., pp. 39 ff.

Orphic practices. Cf. Plato, *Laws*, 782C.

Orphics and Pythagoreans. Cf. Guthrie, *The Greeks and their Gods*, pp. 311, n. 3, and 317.

97. Cyclops, 646.

98. Leotychidas. Cf. Plutarch, *Apoph. Lac.*, 224E; Linforth, op. cit., pp. 233 ff.

Theseus. Cf. Euripides, *Hippolytus*, 952 f.

Eurydice. Cf. Euripides, *Alcestis*, 357 ff.; Plato, *Sympos.*, 179D; Isocrates, XI, 7; Guthrie², *Orpheus*, pp. 29 ff., 44; Linforth, op. cit., p. 31.

99. Titans. Cf. Guthrie, op. cit., pp. 174 ff.; Linforth, op. cit., pp. 339 ff.

Myths. Cf. Marót, *Die Anfänge der Griechischen Literatur*, p. 184.

Thrace. Cf. Guthrie, *The Greeks and their Gods*, p. 314.

100. Soma Sema. Cf. Pindar, *fgm.* 131; Plato, *Cratylus*, 400 B.C.; *Republic*, II, 364 E3–365 A3; Nilsson, *Geschichte²*, I, p. 694.

Mud. Cf. Guthrie, *Orpheus²*, pp. 160 ff; Dodds, *Gorgias*, p. 296.

Ancient Grief. Cf. Rose in *Greek Poetry and Life*, pp. 79 ff.

101. Zagreus. Cf. Aeschylus, *fgm.* 228; Guthrie, op. cit., note 36 to Chapter IV, p. 146; Rose, loc. cit., pp. 88 ff.

Theogony. Cf. Guthrie, op. cit., pp. 71 ff.

102. Creator. Cf. Guthrie, op. cit., pp. 81, 106.

Night. Cf. Cornford, *CQ*, XVII, p. 5.

Time. Cf. Kirk and Raven, *Presocratic Philosophers*, p. 39, n. 1.

Orphic literature. Cf. Linforth, op. cit., pp. 139 ff.

Egg. Cf. Nilsson, *HThR*, XXVIII, 1935., pp. 199 ff.; Pollard, *AJP.*, 1948, p. 374 (*Birds*, 690 f.). But cf. Thomas, *Epekeina*, pp. 43 ff.

103. Delphi. Cf. Rose, loc. cit., p. 86.

Sun Apollo. Cf. Euriphides, *fgm.* 781, 11 f.; *Catasterismi*, 24.

104. Orphics and Pythagoreans. Cf. Wilamowitz, *Glaube*, II, p. 199; Linforth, op. cit., pp. 252 ff. The recent discovery of Orphic papyri in Thessaly and Macedonia came too late to be discussed here. Cf *Deltion*, XIX (1964), pp. 17 ff.

CHAPTER VI

SEERS, SIBYLS AND SHAMANS

The sixth century B.C. was an era characterized both by psychic and intellectual unrest when the utterances of prophets were believed to be inspired, and the miraculous feats of shamans were generally accepted. Best known of the former were the oracles of Bacis and the Sibyl who, whether historical persons in origin or mere generic titles attached to a class of individuals who claimed to possess a direct approach to god, are yet of importance as being typical of the kind of authority to which men appealed during the ferment and uncertainty of a period as yet uninfluenced by the beginnings of rational thought.

Bacis, like Musaeus, is little more than a name to which the authorship of oracles was conveniently referred. Men naturally turn to seers in times of crisis, so it was only to be expected that the pronouncements of the best known legendary prophet should have been widely quoted and credited during the Persian War. According to Herodotus the Euboeans were warned by Bacis to evacuate their island, a piece of practical advice which they had ignored to their peril, while the accuracy of his forecasts concerning Salamis so impressed the historian that he is constrained to confess: 'When I look to this and perceive how clearly Bacis spoke, I neither venture myself to say anything against prophecies, nor do I approve of others impugning them.' There existed then, if Herodotus' sources are accurate, a corpus of oracles which were referred to Bacis at the end of the sixth century B.C. Their provenance is unknown, though it seems highly likely that they derived from the collection assembled by Pisistratus in the temple of Athena Polias, as the tyrant earned the sobriquet of 'Bacis' himself. That the oracles were shamelessly interpolated or manipulated in order to give events a turn to the Pisistratids' advantage is not proved by the example of Onomacritus. When the latter was detected by Lasus, Pindar's master, inserting a prophecy into the canon of Musaeus, Hipparchus, although he had been his friend, had the forger exiled. Doubtless the library of oracles was sufficiently comprehensive to suit most occasions before the tyrants' fall, and it was only when they were driven to seek sanctuary at Xerxes' court that they took advantage of Onomacritus' lack of scruples and furnished the king with the type of oracles best calculated to tempt him to invade Greece.

The female counterpart of Bacis was Sibylla, whose name and origin alike have resisted analysis. She is first described by the philosopher Heraclitus 'with raging lips uttering prophecies grave, stark and unadorned'. At some stage she was pluralized, but all her early associations are with the east, whether Phrygia, Babylonia, Libya or the Troad. Being legendary figures the dates of the various Sibyls are obscure, and vary in the authorities from the pre-Trojan era to the time of Solon. Best known in later times was the Erythraean Sibyl, whose cave in Asia Minor has been discovered, but it is perhaps not without significance that the oracles quoted all refer simply to a single prophetess. Herodotus curiously ignores them, though we know that they were extant in Aristophanes' time, and that Plato was familiar with their author. Heraclitus again is good evidence for their existence at the close of the sixth century B.C., and although Pausanias' statement that she predicted that the battle between the Lacedaemonians and Argives for Thyreatis in 548 B.C. would end in a stalemate, though vitiated by confusion with the event of 414 B.C. is of interest as the only oracle quoted for the Sibyl at such an early period. Again it seems likely that the Sibylline tradition moved west with the colonizers, and so reached Cumae and Delphi too. It cannot of course be proved that the story that the Sibyl had prophesied at Delphi is very old, yet, if we may judge from Heraclitus, the reputation of the legendary prophetess was such that the Delphians could not have afforded to scorn a tradition that was so well calculated to bolster the oracle's fame. Whether the Sibyl was a female shaman, or whether she had always claimed to be inspired by Apollo, we do not know. The Delphians however would have had no doubts upon the matter, and the dogma was soon accepted that the Sibyl had visited and prophesied at all the leading Apolline centres in Asia and Greece.

Less vague than Bacis and the Sibyl, though still often quasi-legendary and hard to date, were prophets like Cydas the Arcadian (also known as Aletes, the Wanderer, who was surnamed 'Bacis', and said once to have cured the Lacedaemonian women of madness), Euvenius of Apollonia, Lysistratus of Athens, and many more. Of Lysistratus Herodotus reports that he prophesied the wreck of the Persian navy on the Colian strand many years before the battle of Salamis, while Euvenius too was a sixth century seer, father of the soothsayer Deiphonus who accompanied the Corinthians during the Persian War. He belonged to the authentic tradition of Teiresias, for according to legend he was blinded by his countrymen as a punishment for falling asleep while guarding the sacred flock, with the result that his charges were decimated by a pack of marauding wolves. When the surviving sheep became barren the oracles at Delphi and Dodona both warned the Apollonians to grant Euvenius whatever he wished. He demanded a farm and house as compensation, though he was not informed that the citizens were acting in accordance with the oracles' instructions. Though angry when he discovered how he had been tricked Euvenius immediately began to prophesy.

More authentic than any of the foregoing was Amphilytus the Acarnanian. When Pisistratus returned from exile for the second time he landed with his supporters near Marathon, encamping near the temple of Athena at Pallene before marching on Athens. 'Here,' according to Herodotus,' a certain soothsayer, Amphitrytus, an Acarnanian, moved by a divine impulse, came into the presence of Pisistratus, and approaching him uttered this prophecy in the hexameter measure:

> Now has the cast been made, the net is out-spread in the water,
> Through the moonshiny night the tunnies will enter the meshes.

Such was the prophecy uttered under a divine inspiration. Pisistratus, apprehending its meaning, declared that he accepted the oracle, and instantly led on his army.'

The oracle in question could have been interpreted in various ways, and was suited to various events, as the soothsayer was doubtless aware, and this vagueness of reference seems to have been characteristic of oracles in general. Nevertheless the fact that the tyrant accepted it and immediately acted on it shows that in matters of superstition the powerful and unscrupulous were as

credulous as the rest. It also affords an additional reason for supposing that Pisistratus collected oracles not so much to influence
events as to provide a handy means of guidance to his own political
future.

Distinct from the prophets, though often credited with mantic
powers, were shamans like Abaris the Hyperborean and Aristeas
of Proconnesus, who were able to quit their bodies at will.
Shamans are familiar phenomena in modern Mongolia and Tibet,
where adepts still claim the power to make lengthy psychic journeys, so it is perhaps significant that Abaris is called a Hyperborean, one that is who learned the art in the northern hinterland
beyond the Black Sea which had long been associated with Apollo
himself. He flourished, according to lexicographer Harpocration,
quoting Pindar, in the time of Croesus, and travelled round the
world bearing a golden arrow, Apollo's emblem, without ever
once eating food. Even Herodotus scoffs at the story, but then he
was unacquainted with the powers of shamans. According to
the Souda, Abaris visited Athens, while at Sparta he performed
sacrifices as a cure for plagues, and was said to have founded the
shrine of Kore the Saviour. But then shamans were medicine-men
as well as psychic wanderers, and the wondrous tales of their
cures soon became widespread.

Aristeas was a shaman who did not die, but vanished for long
intervals before reappearing alive and well. Reports of his activities vary, but according to Herodotus, who heard the story both
in Cyzicus and Proconnesus, Aristeas fell dead in a fuller's booth.
'The report of the death had just spread through the town, when
a certain Cyzicenian, lately arrived from Artaca, contradicted the
rumour, affirming that he had met Aristeas on his road to Cyzicus
and had spoken with him. This man, therefore, strenuously denied
the rumour; the relatives, however, proceeded to the fuller's
shop with all things necessary for the funeral, intending to carry
the body away. But on the shop being opened no Aristeas was
found, either dead or alive. Seven years afterwards he reappeared,
they told me, in Proconnesus, and wrote the poem called by the
Greeks 'The Arimaspeia' after which he disappeared a second time.'

Later still he turned up in Italy, significantly enough in the city
of Pythagoras. Aristeas then, as the Metapontines affirm, appeared
to them in their own country, and ordered them to set up an altar
in honour of Apollo, and to place near it a statue to be called that

of the Proconnesian. 'Apollo,' he told them, 'had come to their country once, though he had visited no other Italiots, and he had been with Apollo at the time, not however in his present form, but in the shape of a crow.' Having said so much he vanished.

The ability to assume animal or bird form is claimed by medicine-men the world over, and the association of Aristeas with the fabulous northern Arimaspi likewise suggests his shaman descent. During his travels too he was said to have been possessed by Apollo, to indicate that his journeys were taken by supernormal means. The poem on the Arimaspi was written apparently after the Cimmerian invasion so Aristeas has been referred to the seventh century B.C. But rumours respecting his continued survival were clearly extant in the sixth.

Hermotimus of Clazomenae possessed similar powers till his enemies effectively put an end both to him and them by burning the shaman's body while his soul was still absent. The most famous of all was Epimenides the Cretan. He too, like Abaris, is said to have flourished in the time of Croesus, though according to Plato he prophesied at Athens and performed religious rites in 500 B.C. But then he once slept for fifty-seven years, and was credited with having lived for almost three centuries. Among other places he purified the isle of Delos, and was also responsible for ridding Athens of the evil hauntings which befell after the treacherous murder of the Cylonian conspirators. There he is said to have practised chthonian rites, and even to have offered human sacrifice. As with the Sibyl, Herodotus is silent on the subject of Epimenides so that for our knowledge of him we are forced to rely on late sources. Most of these are vitiated by myth and *Märchen*, yet the residue suggests that a medicine-man called Epimenides once existed and was credited with abnormal powers. His association with Crete is certainly not in the true shaman tradition, but the island was always one of mystery for the Greeks and legend told how Apollo himself had been purified there of blood-guilt after slaying the Python. According to Plutarch Epimenides was known as the 'New Cures', which suggests that he was regarded as having been initiated into the mysteries of the semi-divine Curetes, who were reported to have protected and fed the infant Zeus, or his chthonian Cretan counterpart. Finally he came to be regarded as the author of a Theogony of an antiquity even more dubious than his own.

Though usually regarded as a philosopher, Pythagoras of Samos was in many ways the greatest of the *Wundermänner*. Attempts at any rate were made in ancient times to bring him into association with Abaris, Aristeas and Epimenides as well as several other legendary miracle-workers, while his doctrine of transmigration had much in common with shamanism. Despite these claims Pythagoras might well seem out of place in a treatise on Greek religion. But that he regarded himself as a religious innovator there can be no doubt, or that he shared a common background of beliefs with the followers of Orpheus.

The historical facts concerning him, though often obscure in detail, are generally not disputed. Born about 570 B.C. in Samos, he moved west during the second half of the sixth century to Croton in south Italy, perhaps to escape the tyranny of Polycrates. That the order which he founded there was no mere brotherhood of intellectuals is clear from the long list of tabus which the members were bound to observe. Indeed it bore a closer resemblance to a religious seminary than to a normal philosophical school. According to Iamblichus the Pythagoreans were bound to observe all the familiar Orphic canons against flesh-eating, contamination with the dead or with plants or objects associated with death, against entering temples in unclean robes, or defiling them with childbirth or blood. In the latter eventuality the defilement had to be expunged with sea-water or gold. More homely rules included the warning, familiar from Hesiod, against bathing in water defiled by women, and the famous interdiction against over-indulgence in beans. Such were the rules of the society which though largely borrowed from ordinary folk tabus had never before, apart from the Orphics, formed the basis of a way of life. Possibly or even probably Pythagoras borrowed the entire system from the Orphics, though this has been denied, and Detienne has recently claimed to have recognized Pythagorean traits in the Homeric heroes. Nevertheless there was one major difference. The Orphics with their crusade against the blood-guilt of the omophagia were primarily concerned with tabus, whereas Pythagoras was a prophet of the science of numbers.

To claim that Pythagoras actually discovered mathematics is going too far. Mathematical systems had been known to the Egyptians and Babylonians from time immemorial. The Greeks' unique contribution was to raise the science from a rule of thumb method to something which bid fair to unlock the key of the universe. The sudden realization of the potentialities of mathematics proved so overwhelming that Pythagoras was content to explain everything in its terms. It is doubtful, of course, whether he advanced very far on the pure mathematical plane. He was more concerned with the properties of the *tetractys*, the mystical triangle whose sum was ten. Coming as he did from the neighbourhood of Ionia it would have been strange had he not been influenced by the speculations of the early physicists. Each claimed in turn to have discovered the basic principle of the cosmos, and Pythagoras proffered his own theory too. It was, he said, the monad, the principle of unity which formed the apex of the triangle. Starting from this 'First Unit' he attempted to explain the existence of the varying natural phenomena. For this his followers were severely censured by Parmenides, himself said to have been a pupil of the Pythagoreans Diochaetes and Ameinias, who charged them with logical inconsistency. But to have advanced such arguments against Pythagoras himself would have been anachronistic and meaningless. Indeed it is significant that Parmenides never mentions the number theory at all, but contents himself with assailing the Pythagorean philosophy in general terms.

The prime difference between the attitudes of the Ionian physicists and that of the Pythagoreans *vis-à-vis* religion was that whereas the former sought to replace traditional beliefs altogether the latter, like the Orphics, were religious reformers whose love of wisdom and philosophy grew out of their way of life. They aimed in fact to become the philosopher saints of a pre-Platonic Republic. That they failed in practice was perhaps not so much due to their innate incompetence as to the inevitable jealousy of their fellow men. Whether Pythagoras himself was concerned with founding an ideal state we do not know, for his aims were kept secret. What may be deduced is that the founder of the order was an ardent prophet who regarded his knowledge, and possibly even himself, as semi-divine. '*Autos epha*—he himself said', was the ultimate authority of the *akousmatikoi*, literally 'those willing to hear', the elder disciples, who were more concerned with the observance of the canons of the order than with the investigation of the mathematical principles—the concern of the *mathematikoi* —on which the new philosophy rested. They and their master were in fact genuine religious mystics rather than mathematicians in any real sense.

That Pythagoras attempted to reform and not to attack established dogma is clear from his attitude to the Apolline religion. In it he observes all that was best in Greek religious belief, and his followers adopted it as their own. It was doubtless the Apolline religion in its purest form as found at Delphi that most appealed to the Pythagoreans, and so closely did the founder hold to its tenets that he was known as 'the son of Apollo', and was actually identified with the god himself. This tendency to monism was, as Cornford pointed out, doubtless due to the breakdown of the clan system during the sixth century B.C. Hitherto men had worshipped the gods which traditionally favoured or protected their family or tribe. Once they had broken away from such ties they were free to choose a deity of their own seeking which in the case of ascetics like the Pythagoreans was bound to be Apollo. The Pythagoreans were in fact doubly estranged from their ancestral beliefs in that they had voluntarily removed to a foreign country. Also having not emigrated to the west as ordinary colonists they were under no obligation to continue worshipping the gods of their home-state. At the same time religious independence involved personal responsibility too. Hitherto blood-guilt had been shared by the community at large. Now the individual was called upon to purge himself. This he could achieve by undergoing ritual initiation into the Pythagorean order, which from one point of view replaced the tribe. Insistence on the doctrine of transmigration meant that the Pythagorean, unlike the ordinary Greek, was bound to respect life in all its forms. The natural result was that he was regarded as a crank and his views, like those of Socrates later, lent themselves not infrequently to unjust ridicule, as e.g. when the religious critic Xenophanes says that Pythagoras once reprimanded someone for beating a puppy because he recognized a friend's voice in its howls. But behind it all was a kind of pantheism, which Pythagoras expressed as the principle of order. But order implies disorder, and the purity of the good life lived according to the akousmata logically necessitated the concept of evil. It was, of course, this implied dualism that Parmenides attacked, though Pythagoras does not appear to have been much troubled by the logical dilemma.

Pythagoras, like the seers and shamans before him, aimed at

soul-mastery which he equated with the attainment of that purity of mind which was characteristic of the worship of the Hyperborean Apollo. In order to realize this aim he and his followers were prepared to undergo bodily privation. The body, as the Orphics held, was a tomb, which had to be mastered. Once that hard victory was won them everything else followed. The soul, meantime, like that of Epimenides, spent its time in *theoria*, the contemplation of the cosmos, which reflected on a large scale the life of man. 'Life,' he said, 'is like a festival; just as some come to the festival to compete, some to ply their trade, but the best people come as spectators, so in life the slavish men go hunting for fame or gain, the philosophers for the truth.' As the soul imitated the divine so the parts of the cosmos were revealed to the contemplators as being attuned to the celestial order. But it is with the Pythagorean view of the individual soul that we are more concerned here. In the celebration of the Dionysiac thiasos each member of the rout gradually lost his psychic entity and became one with the god. He was possessed, as we say, and abandoned himself to ecstasy, literally the experience of standing outside himself, which was characteristic of both the shamanistic and Dionysiac religions, except that with the shaman it was an individual exercise and not a phenomenon associated with a group. But the Pythagoreans like the Orphics sought pyschic awareness in another way. The Orphics did so by practising asceticism in accordance with the dogma of soma-sema and the divine spark latent in the Titan myth. The Pythagoreans likewise practised asceticism but in order to increase the soul's awareness of the underlying principles which governed the universe. These were, of course, mathematical, and as such based more firmly on intellect than on emotion. But that the beliefs of the early Pythagoreans were not wholly scientific is clear from their regard for Apollo. Far from being theists, in the Milesian sense, they believed firmly in the deity who dealt in reason as far as any of the Greek gods could.

A notable parallel with Orphic beliefs was, as has been mentioned at the end of the last chapter, the doctrine of harmony which for the Pythagoreans implied the adjustment or attunement of the parts to a whole. The Orphics admittedly never worked out the mathematical intervals of music, but of the religious power of the lyre they were in no doubt. For them it appeared to symbolize the Apolline restraint which could act as a brake on the Dionysiac thiasos. For the Pythagoreans it was a physical representation of the innate harmony which characterized the universe, and which if properly conceived on mathematical principles could unify the opposed conceptions of bounded and unbounded space. As the tuning of the lyre was the outward expression of this harmony, it was employed together with poetry to cure the maladies of the spirit.

Despite Simmias' argument that if the soul represents a harmony of bodily opposites it must cease to exist when the body dies it seems perfectly possible, as Cornford maintained, that the Pythagoreans regarded the principle of harmony itself as immortal. After all it was based, in their view, on universal mathematical principles which neither death nor any other known cataclysm could possibly affect. Whether, as Poseidonius stated, the Platonic doctrine of the tripartite division of the soul actually derived from Pythagoras or not it seems clear that the latter, like the Orphics, was fully aware of the dualism in human nature. The *soma-sema* doctrine itself was in essentials an expression of this conscious duality, which could only be resolved by effecting a reconciliation between the two warring parts. The analogy of these parts with the gods and the beasts, with man as the mean between the two, was alluded to both by Plato and Aristotle in a manner which suggests that they were quoting an earlier and familiar doctrine, which could well have been Pythagorean. Even so we have no means of knowing whether it formed part of the original dogma of the master as expounded to the *akousmatikoi* in the sixth century B.C. Yet the principle of dualism was of such cardinal importance for both the Orphics and Pythagoreans that it can hardly be doubted that its existence was at least implicit in the original systems. What can be legitimately doubted is whether the immortality of the soul was conceived in a philosophical sense in the middle of the sixth century B.C. or only in a physical sense as the survival of life. Here we are handicapped by the absence of contemporary Pythagorean records, and by the inevitable comparisons with developed Platonism. In either event the doctrine of *harmonia* provided a solution in mathematical terms to the new problem of personal immortality, and Pythagoras was the first Greek to regard the human soul as something of moral importance.

NOTES TO CHAPTER VI

Page 106. Bacis and the Sibyl. Cf. Herodotus, VIII, 22, 77; Rohde, *Psyche*, notes 58–65 to Chapter IX; Dodds, *The Greeks and the Irrational*, note 45 to Chapter III; Pollard, *Delphica, BSA*, 55, 1960, pp. 195 ff.

Pisistratus. Cf. Herodotus, V, 90.

107. Erythraean Sibyl. Cf. Buresch, *AM*, 1892, pp. 16 ff.

108. Lysistratus. Cf. Herodotus, VIII, 96.

Euvenius. Cf. Herodotus, IX, 93.

Amphilytus. Cf. Herodotus, I, 62.

109. Abaris, Aristeas. Cf. Herodotus, IV, 13, 36; Rohde, op. cit., note 108 to Chapter IX; Dodds, op. cit., pp. 140 ff.; Bolton, *Aristeas*.

Kore. Cf. Pausanias, III, 13, 2.

Arimaspeia. Cf. Rohde, op. cit., note 112 to Chapter IX; Bowra, 'A Fragment of the Arimaspeia', *CQ*, 1956, pp. 1 ff.

110. Hermotimus. Cf. Rohde, op. cit., note 112 to Chapter IX.

Epimenides. Cf. Plato, *Laws*, 642 D E; Plutarch, *Solon.*, 12; Rohde, op. cit., note 123 to Chapter IX; Guthrie, *Orpheus*, p. 93.

111. Pythagoras. Cf. Dodds, op. cit., p. 143; Morrison, 'Pythagoras of Samos', *CQ*, 1956, pp. 135 ff.; for Iamblichus, cf. Kirk and Raven, *The Presocratic Philosophers*, N. 256.

Orphics. Cf. Kirk and Raven, op. cit., p. 220; Detienne, *Homère, Hésiode et Pythagore*, Brussels, 1962.

112. Monad. Cf. Cornford, 'Mysticism and Science in the Pythagorean Tradition', *CQ*, XVI, 1922, p. 140; XVII, 1923, pp. 6 and 7.

113. Puppy. Cf. Xenophanes, *fgm.* 7; Kirk & Raven, op. cit., pp. 168 ff.

114. Life. Cf. Diogenes Laertius, VIII, 8, translated by Kirk and Raven.

Shamanism and Possession. Cf. Dodds, op. cit., p. 71 and n. 43, p. 88.

115. Space. Cf. Kirk and Raven, op. cit., p. 243.

Simmias. Cf. Plato, *Phaedo*, 85E and 92; Cornford, *CQ*, XVI, p. 146.

Poseidonius. Cf. Burnet, *Phaedo*, note on 68C.

Warring parts. Cf. Plato, *Republic*, 443C; Aristotle, *Eth. Nic.*, I, 13; X, 7, 8; *Politics*, I, 1, 12.

HEROES AND DEMIGODS

—◦❧❦◦—

Herodotus tells a strange story about Cleisthenes, tyrant of Sicyon, who flourished during the first half of the sixth century B.C. 'This king,' he records, 'when he was at war with Argos, put an end to the contests of the rhapsodists at Sicyon, because in the Homeric poems Argos and the Argives were so constantly the theme of song. He likewise conceived the wish to drive Adrastus, the son of Talaus, out of his country, seeing that he was an Argive hero. For Adrastus had a shrine at Sicyon, which yet stands in the market-place of the town. Cleisthenes therefore went to Delphi and asked the oracle if he might expel Adrastus. To this the Pythoness is reported to have answered: "Adrastus is the Sicyonians' king, but thou art only a robber." So when the god would not grant his request, he went home and began to think how he might contrive to make Adrastus withdraw of his own accord. After a while he hit upon a plan which he thought would succeed. He sent envoys to Thebes in Boeotia, and informed the Thebans that he wished to bring Melanippus, the son of Astacus, to Sicyon. The Thebans consenting, Cleisthenes carried Melanippus back with him, assigned him a precinct within the government-house, and built him a shrine there in the safest and strongest part. The reason for his so doing (which I must not forbear to mention) was, because Melanippus was Adrastus' great enemy, having slain both his brother Mecistes and his son-in-law Tydeus. Cleisthenes, after assigning the precinct to Melanippus, took away from Adrastus the sacrifices and festivals wherewith he had till then been honoured, and transferred them to his adversary. Hitherto the Sicyonians had paid extraordinary honours to Adrastus, because the country had belonged to Polybus, and Adrastus was Polybus' daughter's son; whence it came to pass that Polybus, dying childless, left Adrastus his kingdom. Besides other ceremonies, it had been their wont to honour Adrastus with tragic choruses, which they assigned to him rather than Bacchus, on account of his calamities. Cleisthenes now gave the choruses to Bacchus, transferring to Melanippus the rest of the sacred rites.'

Adrastus, king of Argos, was leader of the famous expedition of the Seven against Thebes. He was also a Sicyonian by adoption in as much as his grandfather Polybus, king of Corinth, had included both cities in his domain. Nevertheless, as a former king of Argos, his sympathies were likely to be biased in favour of the foe, and for this reason Cleisthenes was anxious to be rid of him. At the same time he was doubtless well aware of the danger of offending a powerful hero, whose enmity could prove even more distressing than an Argive success. Nevertheless he was an upstart who mocked the Sicyonians by renaming their tribes after asses and swine. Such a man was unlikely to be overscrupulous in his treatment of a Dorian hero, though he was careful to attempt to obtain Delphic sanction for what must have appeared to his contemporaries an unparalleled piece of hybris. When baulked of official approval he fell back on the stratagem of introducing the cult of Melanippus, who had earned, in life, Adrastus' hatred by slaying his son-in-law Tydeus. By so doing he doubtless hoped to counteract Adrastus' capacity for malignity by opposing to it the rival favour of Astacus' son. When the Thebans granted him permission to introduce the cult of Melanippus at Sicyon, he honoured him with a shrine within the seat of government itself. This was to give the new hero an advantage over his rival, whose shrine was further removed from the centre of things. So Adrastus was permitted to remain, deprived of his honours, and the city, as far as we know, suffered no ill. The reference to tragic choruses in connection with Adrastus persuaded the late Sir William Ridgeway that tragedy originated in hero-cults. Though the weight of evidence is against the theory this unique instance has still to be explained.

The extent of Cleisthenes' hybris may be gauged from the circumstance that during the archaic period dead heroes were generally regarded as grim and dangerous doubles of what they had been in life. They were neither the weak phantoms of the Homeric Nekyia, nor the privileged demigods of the Western Isles, and though they appear to have first sprung into prominence during the seventh and sixth centuries B.C. and are not mentioned

directly either by Homer or Hesiod, the belief in powerful ghosts
of a dimly remembered inhumating age did not necessarily die out
with the Dorian invasion. The very existence of the Mycenaean
shaft-tombs in the flanks of the Areopagus had been forgotten by
the Athenians of the classical era. But the beliefs implicit in such
wealthy burials subconsciously lived on, as the discoveries of
hero-shrines at Mycenae prove. Great importance was attached
to the relics of heroes, and their importation into favoured states.
A famous example is Herodotus' story of the removal to Sparta
of the bones of Orestes, in the time of king Croesus. The Delphic
oracle had informed the Spartans that they would never defeat the
Tegeans in battle until the hero's bones had been brought to the
city. The difficulty was to locate Orestes' resting place, as the
clues supplied by the Pythoness were typically obscure. In the end
they were discovered by a smith, while engaged in sinking a well,
and secretly removed by another man who was anxious to in-
gratiate himself with the Spartans. From then on 'whenever the
Spartans and Tegeans made trial of each other's skill in arms, the
Spartans had greatly the advantage'. The coffin in question was,
according to the historian, no less than seven cubits long, and the
body was commensurate, yet despite these pardonable exaggera-
tions the circumstances of the discovery render it highly likely
that the smith had chanced on a Mycenaean tomb. A great king or
warrior was regarded as possessing something very like mana or
imperium in Wagenvoort's sense. When he died the outflow of
mana was regarded as continuing unabated and, provided his tomb
was honoured with appropriate sacrifices, could be canalized for
the benefit of the neighbouring state. Hence an injunction attributed by Porphyry to Draco bade the Athenians 'offer public
worship to the gods and heroes that dwell in the land, according
to ancestral custom'. The normal exclusion of women from
heroes' shrines was probably due to the belief that their presence
was likely to impair the outflow of the heroes' mana, though in
the case of priestesses there was the additional consideration that
all such places were polluted with death.

The task of maintaining good relations with the numerous
minor heroes and heroines of Attic cult fell apparently, even in
archaic times, to the small private organizations known as 'orgeones'. Such heroes as Echelos, the Possessor, of the recently discovered Areopagus inscription, Egretes, the Rouser, Amynos, the

Warder off of evil, and Hypodectes, the Receiver, were, as Ferguson maintains, local deities whose powers could be harnessed by suitable sacrifice. In type they were analogous to the heroes worshipped by the Salaminioi, such as Eurysaces, whose shrine the Eurysakeion has been thought to antedate 508/7 B.C. when the struggle of Athens and Megara for Salamis was ended by arbitration, Ioleos, Nauseiros, Phaiax, Skiros and Teucros, but had much in common with the major heroes whose cults were more naturally a state affair. Famous heroes like Adrastus or Melanippus were honoured with chthonian rites, as they were visualized as dwelling underground, but the ritual attaching to minor powers was not infrequently, as Nock has shown, Olympian in character rather than chthonian. Chthonian rites differed from those reserved for the deities who inhabited the upper air in several important particulars. In the first place a raised altar was dispensed with, and a shallow trench known as an *eschara* was substituted in its place. Into this offerings were poured, so that the entombed hero might enjoy them after they had soaked into the earth. They were sometimes of a bloodless nature even when a warrior was concerned, but when beasts were sacrificed the victims' throats were turned down instead of upward so that the blood could run more easily into the trench. The ritual, known as *enagisma*, was performed in the evening or at night, and the victims were black and of the male sex. The flesh was burned, and only partially shared with the celebrants, though sometimes sacrificial meals were prepared to which the hero was invited as a guest. Apart from some evidence from Pindar, and dramatic scenes in Aeschylus, the details are mainly preserved in later sources, or are supplied by inference. But ritual is essentially conservative, and there is no reason to suppose that it differed greatly in archaic times.

That a hero could chasten as well as favour, if his worshippers failed to behave with becoming propriety, is clear from Herodotus' tale of Talthybius, whose popularity during the archaic period is attested by his appearance on a sixth century relief, as well as in a series of Attic vases. When Darius sent his envoys to Greece demanding earth and water in token of submission, the Athenians hurled them into the Barathron, the Attic equivalent of the Tarpeian rock, while the Spartans threw them into a well. 'On the Lacedaemonians, however,' the historian records, 'the wrath of Talthybius, Agamemnon's herald, fell with violence. Talthybius has a temple at Sparta, and his descendants, who are called Talthybiadae, still live there, and have the privilege of being the only persons who discharge the office of herald. When therefore the Spartans had done the deed of which we speak, the victims at their sacrifices failed to give good tokens; and this failure lasted for a very long time. Then the Spartans were troubled; and, regarding what had befallen them as a grievous calamity, they held frequent assemblies of the people, and made proclamation through the town. "Was any Lacedaemonian willing to give his life for Sparta?" Upon this two Spartans, Sperthias, the son of Aneristus, and Bulis, the son of Nicolaos, both men of noble birth, offered themselves as an atonement to Xerxes for the heralds of Darius slain at Sparta. So the Spartans sent them away to the Medes to undergo death. . . . This conduct on the part of the Spartans caused the anger of Talthybius to cease for a while, notwithstanding that Sperthias and Bulis returned home alive. But many years after it awoke once more, as the Lacedaemonians themselves declare, during the war between the Peloponnesians and the Athenians.'

The slaying of the ambassadors took place admittedly at the beginning of the fifth century, but is good evidence for the manner in which heroes were regarded during the previous years. In this instance a local hero had turned against his own people with the kind of logical impartiality so typical of the Greeks; for having been Agamemnon's herald in life all heralds or ambassadors came automatically under his protection. Obviously he was a hero of powerful mana, whose powers men flouted at their peril.

The spread of hero-cults during the archaic period received a notable stimulus from epic poetry, and association was eagerly sought with the great warriors of popular tradition. Such was the cult of the Telamonian Ajax which seems to have been established early at Salamis, and apparently reached Attica in an ancestral capacity. The grim story of the Locrian maidens in connection with the cult of the Lesser Ajax has already been mentioned, and though the authorities are late Polybius' statement that the supply of maidens antedated the foundation of the colony in Italy suggests that the cult could date, at least, from as early as the eighth century B.C. Its peculiar barbarity is unparalleled in Greece, though the sacrifice of women to heroes is not. Even in Mycenaean times there are indications that the women of the household were put to death when a king or warrior died, and Achilles, according to a story which may derive from the *Nostoi*, the lost epic poem which described the return of the heroes from Troy, prevented the fleet from sailing until his betrothed, the maiden Polyxena, had been sacrificed to appease his ghost. The cult of Achilles appears to have been confined mainly to the region of the Euxine Sea in archaic times. The Achilleion at Leuke was known to Arctinus, a contemporary of Hesiod, and is described in Arrian's Periplus. It contained an ancient wooden image, and consultants at the oracle were advised, in true chthonian fashion, through the medium of dreams. There was also a quaint legend that the sea-birds which thronged there cleaned out the temple every day. On the mainland, though we do not know the dates of their foundation, Achilles was honoured with many shrines. One of the best known was at Brasiae in Laconia, while at Elis and Croton, as at Rhoeteum, wailing by women formed part of the ritual. This was probably done in memory of the original lament for Achilles by his mother Thetis and the sea-nymphs, though it was also a feature of the cults of Medea and Ino-Leucothea, while the tragic choruses performed in honour of Adrastus probably included formal dirges. Women also sacrificed their hair both to heroes and heroines at Troezen, Delos and Megara.

At Delphi the tradition that Achilles' son Neoptolemus, or Pyrrhus, had been slain by a Delphian in a brawl over the flesh of the victim which he was sacrificing was celebrated by Pindar, and was also known to his contemporary Pherecydes. Although it is difficult to decide from the poet's language whether he was referring to the existence of an actual cult, the circumstance that the hero was fated to dwell there suggests that he possessed a tomb, whether situated 'within the ancient grove' or, as Pherecydes reports, within the actual sanctuary. A peribolus, at any rate, has been discovered by the French, superimposed upon earlier structures. It would seem, therefore, that Pyrrhus' tomb was well known in the early fifth century, and by implication in the sixth. Possibly the cult originated at the time of the fall of Crisa, through the influence of Anthela. Pausanias says that the Delphians dishonoured Pyrrhus' tomb until he assisted them against the Gauls.

Among the class of founder heroes Pelops was perhaps the most famous. His cult at Olympia is also referred to by Pindar, and dated, at least, from archaic times.

And now he hath a share in fair blood-offerings, laid to rest by Alpheios' ford. His much-frequented tomb is hard by the altar to which all men come.

The offering of blood-sacrifices was, as we have seen, usual, if not invariable, at a hero's tomb, and is mentioned by Pausanias in connection with Tronis, where the Phocians honoured Xanthippus as the founder of their race. The cult of Pelops was probably at least coeval with the time when the games attained world fame. But if Farnell is right in supposing that traditional oecists were in fact real people, then the likelihood is that its origins were lost in pre-history. The ritual observed at the Pelopium was certainly striking and primitive.

'The victim,' says Pausanias, 'is a black ram. The sooth-sayer receives no share of this offering, but the custom is to present the neck alone of the ram to the woodman, as he is known. The woodman is one of Zeus' servants, and his duty is to supply cities and private individuals with wood for the sacrifices at a fixed cost. The wood is that of the white poplar, and no other kind. Whoever partakes of the flesh of the victim offered to Pelops, whether he be a man of Elis or a stranger, is forbidden to enter the temple of Zeus.'

Here the rites were clearly chthonian, though in this instance the flesh was presumably shared by those taking part in the sacrifice, and not burned entire for the hero's sole benefit. The uncleanness of death also clung to the tomb, and was not permitted to pollute the temple.

Parallel cults to that of Pelops were those of Cadmus at Thebes, Cychreus at Salamis, whose epiphany was a snake, and Phoroneus at Argos, some of which possibly originated with real personages. Indeed the establishment of the cults of historical heroes was by no means unknown during the sixth century B.C. and became comparatively common in late classical times. Herodotus tells in his fifth book how the ill-fated Spartan Dorieus, who went out to found the colony of Heraclea in Sicily, was accompanied by one Philip, the son of Butacidas, a man of extraordinary beauty. He was also an Olympian victor, and when he fell in battle with

Dorieus the victorious men of Egesta 'raised a hero-temple over his grave, and they still worship him with sacrifices'. Later in the same book the historian describes how the Amathusians, during the revolt of Cyprus against Darius, mounted the head of the Carian Onesilus, the author of the revolt, over the city gates. When a swarm of bees settled in the skull they consulted the oracle concerning the omen. That latter replied that they were 'to take down the head and bury it, and thenceforth to regard Onesilus as a hero, and offer sacrifice to him year by year; so it would go the better with them'. This latter event occurred admittedly at the very beginning of the fifth century B.C., and has a parallel in the heroization of the Persian giant Artachaes by Xerxes.

The cults of another class of heroes, who were not, strictly speaking, heroes at all, but local agricultural daemons, were widespread throughout Greece in late classical times, and were probably of ancient origin. Indeed such rustic heroes as Kyamites—Bean-man—whose shrine Pausanias observed on his way to Eleusis Lycus, the Wolf-man, Eunostos—Bringer of good return—who was worshipped at Tanagra in Boeotia, or Boukolos—Neat-herd—who murdered him—and Ochna—Pear-tree—who hanged herself for love of him, have been referred to an ancient stratum of religious belief which antedated even the worship of the Olympian gods. Certainly such divinities as Karpo (Fruitfulness), Thallo (Bloom), Aglauros and Pandrosos (Brightness and hoped-for Universality of Dew), Auxesia (Increase), Eriboea (Richness in Cattle), seem strikingly analogous to such familiar Italian conceptions as Venus, in her original neuter sense, or Robigus who was responsible for the appearance of rust on corn.

Similar in nature to agricultural heroes, though more powerfully personalized, were Echetlaeus of Marathon, the daemon of the plough-handle, who was reputed to have wielded a plough-share against the Persians, Aristaeus, who introduced men to the arts of farming, and Opheltes—Giver of Increase—who was associated with the celebration of the Nemean Games. Opheltes was undoubtedly a fertility daemon in origin, as his name implies, and in legend he was connected with snakes. The Games themselves included chthonian features, for the judges wore dark robes and the parsley-crown awarded to the victors was regarded as a symbol of death. Hence the inference that the Games were founded at a spot where a chthonian cult was already in existence seems virtually inescapable. According to a legend, preserved by Pausanias, Opheltes was bitten by a snake after being set down by his nurse on the grass. The place was marked by his tomb, which was surrounded by a sacred enclosure, and included altars.

The Isthmian Games likewise boasted a child-president in Melicertes, surnamed Palaemon or Wrestler. Melicertes was the son of Ino-Leucothea, in origin an earth-, not a sea-goddess. He was worshipped with chthonian rites as a buried hero, who, like Linus and Hyacinthus, died during the heat of the year. To him offerings were made of black cattle, and he was also honoured with mysteries.

The cult of heroines, although not as popular or widespread as that of heroes, played an important part in Greek religion. Unlike their male counterparts the heroines were in origin usually figures from saga, like Helen or Iphigeneia, or deities like Ariadne, rarely historical persons. Ino was a vegetation goddess in origin, associated in myth with seed-corn. She was said to inhabit the bottom of a deep pool in Laconia, and also had an oracle there. Probably her sea associations developed out of the custom of casting her image periodically into the deep in a hieratic attempt to rejuvenate her waning powers of fertility. Her cult was manifestly a very ancient one, and though we know nothing of its history during the archaic period there can be no doubt that locally she was credited with powerful chthonian powers.

Helen, whether in origin a goddess, or identified with some forgotten deity through the influence of epic, was honoured with many shrines during the classical period throughout Laconia, and also in Attica and Rhodes. Even as early as the sixth century B.C. she was credited at Therapnae with miraculous powers. According to Herodotus, Ariston, king of Sparta, fell in love with the most beautiful woman in the city. As a child she had been ill-favoured, so her nurse had taken her to Helen's temple and besought the heroine to take away her ugliness. 'One day, as she left the temple, a woman appeared to her, and begged to know what it was she held in her arms. The nurse told her it was a child, on which she asked to see it; but the nurse refused; the parents, she said, had forbidden her to show the child to anyone. However the woman would not take a denial; and the nurse, seeing how highly she prized a look, at last let her see the child. Then the woman gently stroked its head, and said: "One day this child shall be the fairest dame in Sparta." And her looks began to change from that very day.' It is a charming tale, and contains this much truth, that any nurse would have believed at the time in question that the stigma of ugliness could be removed by Helen. And again, of course, it is a fact that ill-favoured children not infrequently become handsome when adult. The nurse, as so often, preferred to approach the less august, but according to popular tradition, far more efficacious heroine, rather than one of the more awful and remote Olympians.

'My own opinion is,' says Herodotus, 'that those Greeks act most wisely who build and maintain two temples of Heracles, in the one of which the Heracles worshipped is known by the name of Olympian, and has sacrifice offered to him as an immortal, while in the other the honours paid are such as are due to a hero.'

Heracles himself belonged neither to the class of ancestral heroes nor to that of the warriors of epic. His cult, indeed, approached more nearly to that of a god, and was associated with a type of hero-shrine peculiar to him alone, consisting of a pediment and pillars, without a roof. From it all women were firmly excluded, though female slaves were admitted at Erythrae and Cos and his priests wore female attire in memory of his sojourn among Thracian women. Offerings of bull's or ox blood, as well as that of rams, boars or cocks, were made to him, and at Lindos in Rhodes the beasts were taken from the plough and immolated with curses. Originally, as we gather from Archilochus' triumph-chant, quoted by Pindar, Heracles was the patron of warriors,

> *Huzza—all triumphant—*
> *Hail, Heracles, king,*
> *Thyself and Iolaos, spearmen twain.*
> *Huzza—all triumphant—*
> *Hail, Heracles, king.*

and such characteristic epithets as *soter*, 'saviour', *apotropaios* and *alexikakos*, 'averter of evil', which were later applied to him referred to this power to ward off death in war. Probably this was still their main significance throughout the sixth century B.C. though they soon acquired a more general connotation. The kind of portrait of Heracles we have in the *Alcestis* was not something

new. The mighty deeds of the insuperable warrior, which were
recorded so vividly by the painters of the black-figure vases, were
familiar to everyone during the archaic period, and men often
found it easier to turn to the genial and approachable hero for
succour than to one of the major deities. For Heracles was regarded as more human than god-like with all an ordinary man's
weaknesses on a heroic scale. Whether he appeared in the guise
of a patron of bastards at Cynosarges, as a murderer who did
penance by suffering serviture, or the humble protector of the
farmers' fruit-trees, he excited a sense of fellow-feeling denied to
the great Olympians. He had suffered greatly, so his sympathies
were wide, and had finally attained apotheosis. So men turned to
him to assist them in their everyday troubles, and worshipped
him universally as 'protector from ill.'

In some ways the most typical heroes of all were Castor and
Pollux. They had already become heroized in the *Odyssey*, where
they are described as the sons of Tyndareus and Leda. Like
Heracles they performed many spectacular feats, and though
regarded as gods, tended to be treated with familiarity. Their
earliest associations, whatever their much disputed origin, was
mainly with Laconia, but also with neighbouring Messenia and
Argos. Sparta herself, according to Pausanias, possessed a sanctuary of the Dioscuri, as well as a separate sanctuary and tomb of
Castor, the mortal twin. The shrine of Pollux stood near a spring
on the road to Therapnae, near which again stood a building
known as the Phoebaeum, which included a shrine of both the
Twins. This building was most probably connected with Phoebe,
an ancient goddess who was connected both in myth and ritual
with the Leucippides, the daughters of Leucippus, who became
the heroes' brides.

The separate worship of the twins was, as Farnell points out, no
more unusual than that of Demeter and Kore, though basically
they were inseparable. Whether chthonian rites were performed
at Castor's tomb we do not know, but the circumstance that it
was conveniently localized in Sparta leads to the suspicion that
it was not very old. Besides, Argos also claimed his tomb, and
honoured him under the title of 'Founder of the Race'. A sixth
century relief in the Spartan museum depicts the twins as spear-
men, standing before two jars. Above them two snakes touch an
egg which occupies the central gable. This, Farnell contends, could

hardly be Leda's egg, as the stories of their birth on the island of Paphos or on Taygetus, make no mention of the egg, which first appears in a scholium to the Hellenistic poet Lycophron. As an egg appears in conjunction with a snake on a separate Spartan relief, he considers that it represents an offering to a dead hero whose familiar was a snake. Farnell's determination never to joust at windmills seems sometimes to lead him too far in the opposite direction. Though the snakes are patent proof of chthonian associations, one cannot help suspecting, in view of the legend, that the remarkable prominence given to the egg signified something more than an offering. What this may have been we do not know, but it seems at least possible that it was the occasion of the legend of the swan-egg laid by Leda which is as old as the *Cypria*.

The Twins were represented ironically by the mysterious *dokana*, two upright beams joined at each end. The earliest extant example dates from the fifth century B.C. and is depicted in association with snakes. Others figure amphorae in addition, to one of which a snake is rearing. From this it has been deduced that offerings were made at the various *anakeia*, as the shrines of the Dioscuri (alias Anakes, the plural of anax, a word used from Mycenaean times with the significance of lord or master), were known, in amphorae, and that the mounds over their tombs were surmounted with *dokana* as the symbol of indissoluble unity. What part the legend that they lived and died alternately played in the ritual may only be surmised, though as Homer knew of it and Pindar featured it it was probably not ignored. Neither do we know whether Herodotus' reference to the Spartan custom of sending images of the Dioscuri with their two kings to war presupposed any primeval association between the kings, themselves descended from twins, and the local heroes, who were cast in the rôle of 'Noblest Saviours' as early as Terpander. Certainly the Aeacidae were summoned from Aegina to assist at Salamis, while the local Delphic heroes Phylacus, who guarded the entrance by the shrine of Athena Pronaea, and Autonous, helped to demoralize the Persians. The Locrians again kept a place for the Lesser Ajax in their ranks, and the Dioscuri themselves assisted at the battle of Sagra in which the Locrians besieged the men of Croton.

The familiar connection of Castor and Pollux with the constellations cannot, on the present evidence, be proved to antedate the fifth century B.C. But the author of the second Hymn to the Dioscuri knew them in that rôle, as did Euripides, and as heroic functions do not develop overnight it seems fair to assume that this curious association began during the archaic period. Saviours in battle could, as with Heracles, become saviours in general, and the powers of land heroes came to be identified, by a process which is still obscure, with the stars which directed the courses of mariners at sea. The electrical phenomena which occasionally played about the masts and rigging of the merchants' ships also came to be regarded as the outward manifestation of the physical presence of the Twins, whose functions are described so graphically by Alcaeus.

> Come hither forsaking Pelop's isle,
> Doughty sons of Zeus and Leda,
> Show yourselves propitious, Castor
> And Pollux,
>
> Who across the broad earth and all the sea
> Go on swift steeds,
> And easily save men from death
> That freezes,
>
> Leaping on the tops of well-benched ships
> Shining from afar as you run up the rigging,
> And in the grim night bringing light
> To the black ship.

Their subsequent identification with the Great Gods of Samothrace, the Cretan divinities called Kuretes, or the frenzied Corybantes who were priests of Cybele in Phrygia, was an inevitable consequence of this extension of their sphere.

Like Heracles the Dioscuri were privileged to attain something approaching apotheosis, but that this happy event occurred relatively late in their career seems clear from a scholium on Pindar's tenth Nemean ode, which apparently derives from Ibycus. So at Argos and elsewhere where they were worshipped together under the title of Anakes or Anaktes—Lords—an appropriate enough designation for heroes, Farnell supposes, with probability, that their worship was not chthonian, but Olympian.

As warriors it was natural that the Twins should favour

athletes, and several Argolic inscriptions dating from the sixth century B.C. refer to dedications by successful athletes to the Anakes. At Olympia, too, they possessed an altar by the start of the horse-race, where, according to Pindar, they managed the Games in company with Hermes and Heracles. In Athens the Twins were honoured as athletes in the Anakeion, and were provided with meat-dishes and a company of cronies in the festival called *Theo-xenia* or Divine Guests. So much, at least, we learn from Athenaeus, who is quoting from an inscription possibly preserved by Philochorus. Dining with heroes, as Nock points out, shows that the Greeks harboured little sense of repugnance for dwellers in the underworld. The dedication of a bronze discus to the 'Sons of great Zeus', possibly from Cephallenia, is remarkable evidence that the cult of the Tyndaridae had spread as far as the western islands by 600 B.C. The early diffusion of the cult in the north is likewise attested by Simonides, who paid tribute to the Twins, as has already been mentioned, for preserving his life when Scopas' house, at which he was dining, collapsed upon the guests. There is also reason to believe that it had also reached the Thracian Chersonese by the sixth century B.C.

The sixth century also witnessed the spread of the cults of sacral heroes or demigods, like Amphiaraus, Trophonius and Asclepius. The first was identified with the warrior-seer, who was persuaded by his wife, who had been bribed by a necklace, to take part in the disastrous expedition of the Seven against Thebes. He possessed an oracle near Thebes in archaic times, which is mentioned by Herodotus and was celebrated by Pindar. According to the historian its fame was such that Croesus sent his emissaries there, and the replies they brought back satisfied him of its truth. Thither too Mys, Mardonius' agent, was despatched and, being a foreigner, was permitted to pass the night in the Amphiaraion. This, we are told, he was privileged to do, though the Thebans themselves had voluntarily forfeited the right by electing, in response to an oracle, to have Amphiaraus as an ally rather than as a prophet. Of the ritual practised at the Amphiaraion we are not informed, but later at Oropus, on the Boeotian-Attic border, to a spot near which the oracle was moved at the end of the fifth century B.C., consultants after submitting to ritual purification lay down on a ram's skin in the shrine. There they were visited by prophetic dreams which provided answers to their queries. Here too Amphiaraus attained the status of a god, but his original status seems clear from the existence of his ancestral cult at his home in Argos, as well as his worship at Sparta and Phlious, where he was first supposed to have divined by dreams.

Incubation, a thoroughly chthonian feature, was notably practised at the oracle of Trophonius, whose name means 'Nourisher', at Lebadeia in Boeotia. The shrine itself has disappeared, but the cult doubtless developed in association with the springs of Memory and Forgetfulness, which fertilized this barren stretch of land. In Pausanias' day the elaborate ritual included purification, nocturnal anointing, a visit to the springs to achieve forgetfulness of the past, and memory of the things to be revealed, prayer to an ancient image, traditionally fashioned by Daedalus, the legendary Cretan master, and finally descent into a marble chasm. In the chasm was a hole into which the consultant insinuated himself with difficulty, and, after spending the night there, returned feet first. When he emerged he was closely questioned by the priests, respecting all he had seen and done, and then escorted to the house of Good Fortune and the Good Daemon. Pausanias adds that he does not write from hearsay, but had himself undergone the ritual prescribed. Though we have no information respecting the ritual adopted at the oracle in arachaic times, we know at least that it was in operation in the time of Croesus. The consultant would have doubtless purified himself in the spring, as others did in Castalia at Delphi, and then after entering a natural chasm, later shored up with masonry, would have descended into a hole in the earth.

Later the cult appears to have been contaminated with that of Asclepius, though originally they had only the chthonian element in common. Trophonius was a prophet. Asclepius concerned himself with medical cures.

The cult of Asclepius did not, apparently, attain universal popularity until the later fifth and fourth centuries B.C., but his legend is at least as old as Homer, where the physicians Machaon and Podaleirius are described as being his sons. The discovery of a bronze statuette, however, in the vicinity of Corinth or Megara dating possibly from 500 B.C., though the evidence collected by Dr Jeffery suggests that it might well be later, could be evidence that Asclepius was revered as a healing power far from his original home as early as the sixth century B.C. Hitherto men had turned to local heroes like Amynos, Machaon, Oresinus, Podaleirius or Polemocrates, when they sought medicinal cures, but even in Homer they were thought to derive their powers from the hero of Tricca, whose cult did not reach Athens until 420 B.C. Pausanias regarded the image in the sanctuary of Asclepius at Titane as being of primitive type. 'It is impossible,' he says, 'to learn of what wood or metal the image is made, nor do they know who made it, though one or two refer it to Alexanor (son of Machaon who, according to tradition, had founded the northern Peloponnesian cult) himself. Only the face and the hands and the feet of the image are visible, for a white woollen shirt and a mantle are thrown over it.' But as Edelstein pointed out, only the oldest deities were represented undraped, and there are other reasons for doubting Farnell's assumption that the cult at Titane was old. The sacrificial details are nevertheless significant, as being of the regular chthonian type. 'All the portions of the victims which they offer they burn on the ground, except birds, which they burn on the altars.' Incubation, too, was practised as with Trophonius and all earth daemons, and consultants' inquiries were answered through the medium of prophetic dreams.

At Tricca in Thessaly, where, if the cult did not actually originate it was politically assumed that it did, there was a subterranean shrine. There doubtless consultants entered or offered sacrifice, as later they cast offerings into the pit near the Asclepieion in Athens. Asclepius too had a snake as his familiar, and was also represented with dogs. The latter were, as we have seen, also associated with Hecate, whose cult was also Thessalian in origin, but the probability is that Asclepius took them over from Apollo Maleatas. The latter was a hunter and the Asclepieion at Epidaurus stood at the foot of the hill called Kynortion—Hounds-hunting—site of the ancient worship of Maleatas whose place the demigod had usurped. He was also associated, in a subordinate capacity, with Maleatas at Tricca.

Unlike other heroes, Asclepius appears to have been honoured entirely with animal sacrifices, though the goat was tabu. He is therefore sharply separated from the powers of vegetation, as offerings of cereals or fruits had no place in his worship. Though said to be Apollo's son, his only close association with other deities are with such vague powers as Hygieia (Health), Iaso (Healing), and Panakeia (Remedy). When his cult reached Phocis, presumably in the sixth century B.C., the Delphic priests characteristically included it in the Apolline tradition, and the story was current in the time of Pherecydes that Asclepius restored the dead to life at Delphi. Asclepius' later connection with manumission, which was also practised at Delphi, suggests the existence of the kind of intimacy between the demigod and his worshippers that has already been noticed with other heroes. That he came in time to be regarded as a god there seems to be no doubt, but originally he was simply a chthonian daemon especially credited with powers of healing. He was worshipped by the Phocians under the style of 'Founder', which suggests that he may have been introduced by immigrants in the capacity of an ancestral hero too.

At Epidaurus the cult of Asclepius cannot be proved to have existed much before 500 B.C., the dates of the altar and sanctuary. Again no certain likenesses of the god antedate the fifth century B.C. and the most likely inference seems to be that the worship of Asclepius was established at Epidaurus, probably towards the end of the six century B.C., in association, as at Tricca, with the older cult of Apollo Maleatas. At the same time the mere fact of its introduction there suggests that it had already achieved wide fame.

The cult of Asclepius on Cos, though famous from the time of the physician Hippocrates, was undoubtedly powerfully influenced by Epidaurus. That there was some ritual association between the two states is indicated by Pausanias, who describes how a party of Epidaurians touched at Epidaurus Limera in Laconia, and when the snake which they were taking to Cos escaped into a hole they accepted the omen and settled there. In Cos offerings were made to the sacred snake which was kept in an underground chamber, whereas at Epidaurus it was kept in a sanctuary. Direct Thessalian influence cannot be proved either for Epidaurus or Cos, though the legend that Heracles was once victorious over the Meropes has been so interpreted.

The rapid spread of the cult of a new and reputedly efficacious daemon is not difficult to understand. When plagues were raging men were not slow to seek aid in novel quarters, and Athens too turned finally to Epidaurus for help. The demand for a cure of physical pain naturally received priority over purely religious considerations, and during the sixth century B.C., when a new spirit of individualism and enterprise was abroad, the cult of the Triccaean hero, who had long been regarded as the patron of doctors everywhere, was universally acclaimed.

NOTES TO CHAPTER VII

For references to individual heroes, cf. Farnell, *Greek Hero Cults*.

Page 117. Adrastus. Cf. Herodotus, v, 67 f.; Webster, *Greek Art and Literature, 700–530 B.C.*, p. 3.

118. Tragedy. Sir William Ridgeway, *The Origin of Tragedy*.

Heroes. Cf. Nock, 'The Cult of Heroes', *HThR*, XXXVII, 1944; Nilsson, *Geschichte*[2], I, pp. 185, 379, 715.

119. Imperium. Cf. Wagenvoort, *Roman Dynamism*, pp. 59 ff.

Women. Cf. Farnell, *GHC*, pp. 160 ff.

Orgeones. Cf. Ferguson, 'The Attic Orgeones', *HThR*, XXXVII, 1944, pp. 61 ff.; Andrewes, *JHS*, LXXXI, 1961, pp. 1 ff.

Echelos. Cf. Merritt, *Hesperia*, XI, 1942, pp. 282 ff.

120. Salaminioi. Cf. Ferguson, 'The Salaminioi of Heptaphylai and Sounion', *Hesperia*, VII, 1, pp. 1 ff.

Minor heroes. The shrine of Codrus, Neleus and Basile appears to have been post-archaic (cf. Wycherley, 'Neleion', *BSA*, LV, 1960, pp. 61 ff.), though Neleus and Basile could be earlier.

Eschara. Cf. Rohde, *Psyche*, p. 50, note 53 to Chapter I.

Offerings. Cf. Rohde, op. cit., p. 45, note 13 to Chapter I.

Enagisma. Cf. Pindar, *Ol.* I, 90 ff.; *Isth.*, IV, 61 f.; Aeschylus, *Persae*, 607 f.; *Choephoroi*, 124 f.; Rohde, op. cit., p. 140, n. 9.

Talthybius. Cf. Herodotus, VII, 133 f.

121. Ajax. Cf. Pindar, *Nem.*, IV, 47–8; Herodotus, v, 66; Ferguson, *Hesperia*, VII, 1, 1938, pp. 17 ff.

Lesser Ajax. Cf. Polybius, XII, 6.

122. Hair. Cf. Nilsson, *Geschichte*[2], I, p. 137.

Pyrrhus. Cf. Pindar, *Nem.*, VII, 34 f.; Pausanias, X, 24, 6; Fontenrose, *The Cult and Myth of Pyrrhos at Delphi*.

Pelops. Cf. Pindar, *Ol.* I, 146; Pausanias, v, 13, 1 ff.; Drees, *Der Ursprung der Olympischen Spiele*, who regards him as a fertility daemon.

123. Tronis. Cf. Pausanias, X, 4, 10.

Cadmus. Cf. Pausanias, IX, 12, 4.

Cychreus. Cf. Pausanias, I, 36, 1; Ferguson, loc. cit., pp. 17, 20.

Phoroneus. Cf. Pausanias, II, 20, 3.

Dorieus. Cf. Herodotus, V, 49.

124. Amathusians. Cf. Herodotus, V, 114.

Artachaes. Cf. Herodotus, VII, 117.

Kyamites. Cf. Pausanias, I, 37, 4.

Lycus. Cf. Nock, loc. cit., p. 166; Ochna, Plut. Q .G. 300D.

Venus. Cf. Latte, *Römische Religionswissenschaft*, p. 183.

Echetlaeus. Cf. Jameson, 'The Hero Echetlaeus', *Trans. Amer. Philol. Assoc.*, LXXXII, 1951.

Opheltes. Cf. Pausanias, II, 18, 3.

125. Melicertes. Cf. Pausanias, I, 44, 8; II, 2, 1 f.

Ino. Cf. Pausanias, III, 23 f.

Helen. Cf. Theocritus, XVIII, 48; Pausanias, III, 15, 3; 19, 9 and 10; VI, 61; Pollard, *Helen of Troy*, Chapter 7.

126. Heracles. Cf. Herodotus, II, 44; Plutarch, *Quaest. Graec.*, 58, 304CD; Dunbabin, *The Greeks and their Eastern Neighbours*, p. 52.

Archilochus. Cf. Pindar, *Ol.* IX, 1, and scholium.

127. Cynosarges. Cf. Herodotus, VI, 116.

Dioscuri. Cf. Farnell, op. cit., Chapter VIII and refs.; Pollard, ibid.

128. Alternate life and death. Cf. Homer, Od., XI, 298 f.; Pindar, *Nem.*, X, 55 f.; Herodotus, V, 75.

Aeacidae. Cf. Herodotus, VIII, 64.

Phylacus. Cf. Herodotus, VIII, 38, 9.

Constellations. Cf. Euripides, Helen, 1499; Electra, 990; Orestes, 1636–7.

129. Alcaeus. Cf. Bowra, *Greek Lyric Poets*[2], p. 167.

Great Gods. Cf. Hemberg, *Die Kabiren*, p. 268; Lehmann, *Samothrace*.

Curetes. Cf. Pausanias, X, 38, 7.

Corybantes. Cf. Pausanias, III, 24, 3.

130. Theoxenia. Cf. Pindar, *Nem.*, X, 49 f.; Nock, loc. cit., p. 156. Nilsson, *Geschichte*[2], I, pp. 409 ff.

Olympia. Cf. Pindar, *Ol.* III, 33 f.; Pausanias, V, 15, 5.

Amphiaraus. Cf. Pindar, *Ol.* VI, 13; Herodotus, I, 46, 49; Pausanias, IX, 37, 7; 39, 5.

Amphiaraion. Cf. Pausanias, IX, 8, 2.

Croesus. Cf. Herodotus, I, 46.

131. Asclepius. Cf. Homer, II.II, 729.

Statuette. Cf. Roberts, *Epigraphy*, No. 118; Jeffery, *The Local Scripts of Archaic Greece*, p. 130.

132. Titane. Cf. Pausanias, II, 11, 6; Edelstein, *Asclepius*, II, pp. 217 and 240, n. 10.

Tricca. Cf. Edelstein, op. cit., pp. 17–19.

133. Epidaurus. Cf. Edelstein, op. cit., pp. 243–4, 247.

Cos. Cf. Herodotus, VII, 99; Pausanias, III, 23, 6; Edelstein, op. cit., p. 239; Kérenyi, *Asklepios*, p. 52. For view that cult spread from Epidaurus cf. Edelstein, op. cit., pp. 97–101, 238 f.; Roebuck, *Corinth*, XIV, 1951, p. 154. For Pyrrhos as a fire daemon of Marie Delcourt, *Pyrrhos et Pyrrha*, 1965.

CHAPTER VIII

SIRENS

—◦❧❦◦—

There was, as we have seen when considering the claims of seers and shamans to authenticity, an imponderable element in Greek religion which is resistant to logical analysis. Nevertheless even if we do not fully understand the source or manner of divine inspiration its results, in the form of prophecies and miracles, are at least open to inspection for what they are worth. It is otherwise with the Sirens, the curious human-headed birds which are such a familiar feature of archaic monuments, for literature has precious little to say about them, and their history must be studied very largely in art. For all that even Sirens have their importance as the monstrous manifestations of religious notions notoriously hard to express.

The earliest Sirens are, to judge from their beards, preponderantly male, though the earliest of all, from Crete, is beardless and the question of sex is complicated by the fact that women could on occasion wear beards, like the priestess of the Pedasians. Some are furnished with musical instruments and arms to hold them, others appear in musical contexts, while the vast majority are seemingly inserted at the caprice of the artist whether as omens, emissaries, embodiments of power, or purely for decorative purposes. During the sixth century B.C. both armed and unarmed, but increasingly beardless Sirens become common in both mainland and island art, but as Corinth was the chief centre of the ceramic industry during the archaic period, and was also, through her trade, most exposed to oriental influence, many of the more interesting examples appear in Corinthian ware.

The earliest known Corinthian Siren was found at Perachora and is remarkable in that it does not, as so commonly, march with the other creatures in the animal frieze, but alights on the edge like a cheeky sparrow. It is bearded, and so presumably male, and its sphinx-like expression suggests that its presence is not entirely fortuitous, though the riddle behind it we cannot read. Very few Sirens are labelled as such, and when they are the name is applied indifferently to male and female examples alike, without reference to Homer's sea-monsters. Few archaic representations of Odysseus' adventure are known. The Boston Museum of Fine Arts contains a black-figured Corinthian aryballos, dating from the second quarter of the sixth century B.C., which shows two Sirens sitting on a rock with their lips apart singing. The rock is curiously ship-shaped, and to its right appears a rectangular object which Bulle and others have taken to represent Circe's palace. To the right again, though as the vase is round any precise orientation is difficult, is Odysseus' ship and crew with the hero bound to the mast. So far the painting, which, incidentally, is the earliest known, is an accurate enough representation of the Homeric story, but certain other features are difficult to explain. Two enormous birds either hover above or perch on the hurricane-deck, while behind the Sirens a female figure with human form crouches before the rock's phallic-shaped stern. A large fabric(?) conceals the ship's poop, the end of which is curiously fashioned and includes an object shaped like a phallus. If the object is a phallus (and phallic objects are common in Corinthian art), then its presence may be intended to emphasize the Sirens' allure. The birds are probably ornamental and recall scenes on geometric vases. The woman's presence has not been satisfactorily explained. Bulle and others supposed that she represented the Sirens' earth mother Chthon, but the latter does not appear in the *Odyssey*. Müller thought that she was Circe, and that the artist intended her to be associated with the rectangular object and not with the Sirens. But this theory has not found general acceptance because it is based on the hypothetical identification of the rectangular object with Circe's palace. Possibly, of course, the design may not have been intended to represent the Homeric version of the legend at all.

An Attic black-figured lekythos, now in Athens, which dates from the end of the sixth century B.C., shows Odysseus bound to a pillar. Two Sirens perch on rocks on either side of him, one of which is stylized as in previous examples, while the other's wings bear a closer resemblance to those of a real bird. Both are playing musical instruments, while a pair of dolphins sport at the hero's feet. But the absence of a ship is remarkable.

A fragment of a sixth century vase from Naucratis reveals the wing-tip of a Siren diving towards a ship. This has been explained as an early representation of the legend first recorded by Lycophron, and is supported by a later example. A red-figured stamnos, which dates from about 500 B.C., shows Odysseus bound to the mast as his ship passes two rocky bluffs. Upon each of these sits a woman-headed bird, one of which bears the name 'Himeropa'— Enchantment. A third Siren, or perhaps Himeropa imagined as seen at a later stage, plunges into the sea. Her eyes are closed as if in death so the suicide legend appears to date back to an early period, and was, as has been seen, already associated with Orpheus.

In all these examples the Sirens are represented in a familiar context, but elsewhere even as late as the sixth century they have apparently nothing to do either with Odysseus or the sea. Yet that they were regarded as such, for whatever reason, is clear from the examples already mentioned inscribed with the legend 'I am a Siren'.

The monsters on the so-called 'Harpy Tomb' from Xanthos bear the dead in their arms, shrouded like corpses. That they are intended to represent Sirens there seems to be no denying, though their inspiration, which is scarcely surprising considering their provenance, is rather oriental than Greek. A similar monster from Cyprus, dating from the late sixth century, is in the Géau collection. On a Laconian cup in the Louvre collection a bearded figure reclines at the feast, accompanied by winged figures of various types and faced by a Siren. The scene is supposedly a feast of the dead, and the artist, we may infer, is employing the monster to give corporeal form to the notion of other worldliness and the joys of bliss.

Some Sirens are frankly sinister and hard to interpret save as harbingers of doom. Such is the helmeted monster in Karlsruhe, or the one which stands sentry over a prostrate figure on a Corinthian pinax in Berlin. More curious still is the scene depicted on an Attic vase in the Louvre. Theseus is shown slaying the Marathonian bull watched by Aegeus. Above the bull a large Siren stands or hovers with wings outspread facing the hero's father. It is presumably an emissary of some kind from the other world with a message for Aegeus, and is intended to be important as it

dominates the scene. Its precise purport is nevertheless as obscure as that of the monster which flits above the dying Procris in
a fifth century design. Equally mysterious is the Siren which flies
before Anchippus' chariot on an amphora painted by Exekias. In
the context it could represent an evil omen, as Anchippus' ride was
fated to end in disaster, or be an emissary from Hades come to
conduct the hero to the unseen world.

That Sirens were sometimes regarded as representing emissaries or omens or as tokens or familiars of other world powers
seems clear from their association with divinities in general, but
with the more sinister and primeval goddesses in particular.
Proto-Artemis was, to judge from archaic representations, usually visualized as being accompanied by monsters of various types.
But then her lineage was oriental, and even when she yielded
place to the Olympian goddess at the beginning of the sixth century B.C. the latter inherited many of her forebear's features.
Hence when a mirror handle was fashioned in her likeness for
some pretty girl to use, the design included a pair of Sirens, the
charming contemporary counterparts of the grim monsters which
gave visible expression to the primitive forces controlled by the
Mistress of the Beasts. An interesting example dedicated by a
lady called Hippyla to Artemis has recently turned up at Brauron.

The offering of a silver Siren to Hera is recorded in an early
sixth century Samian inscription, and, according to Pausanias, her
statue at Coronea bore Sirens, like the mirror Artemis, in its
hands. It was, he says, a work of the Theban Pythodorus, but he is
at a loss to explain the Sirens' presence. His suggestion that they
were included in memory of the singing contest arranged by Hera
between the Sirens of the Odyssey and the Muses is obviously
advanced *faute de mieux*. An Attic votive tablet dating from the
sixth century B.C. shows the lower half of a deity carrying a Siren
under her wing, but her identity is unknown.

Althena too is accompanied by a Siren, as well as by her owl,
when she is shown setting out in a chariot with her protégé
Heracles on an early red-figured cup in Rome. The owl was, of
course, her personal familiar, but the Siren's presence, unless
it is the visible token of divine protection, is unexplained. In a
chariot scene from Olympia a Siren stands looking back at Apollo,
who is represented with his lyre. Possibly it is intended to per-
sonify the kind of unearthly music that is so movingly described

by Plutarch. He is discussing the curious passage at the end of the Republic where Plato capriciously sets Sirens on the whorls of Necessity instead of Muses, as might have been expected. 'Now Homer's Sirens, it is true, frighten us, inconsistently with the Platonic myth, but the poet too conveyed a truth symbolically, namely that the power of their music is not inhuman or destructive; as souls depart from this world to the next, so it seems, and drift uncertainly after death, it creates in them a passionate love for the heavenly and divine, and forgetfulness of mortality; it possesses them and enchants them with its spell, so that in joyfulness they follow the Sirens and join them in their circuits. Here on earth a faint echo of that music reaches us and, appealing to our souls through the medium of words, reminds them of what they experienced in an earlier existence. The ears of most souls, however, are plastered over and blocked up, not with wax, but with carnal obstructions and affections. But any soul that through innate gifts is aware of this echo, and remembers that other world, suffers what falls in no way short of the very maddest passions of love, longing and yearning to break the tie with the body, but unable to do so.'

Others again pipe for Dionysus and his attendant Satyrs in an early red-figured vase, personifying again possibly the kind of music that could only be heard by adepts in a state of ecstasy. The association of Sirens with other-world joys probably explains their presence on tombs. But the practice did not become widespread until the fifth century B.C. though figures presumably of the deceased appear in scenes with Sirens playing lyres or squatting on pillars.

Many of the earlier Sirens are represented as hostile creatures, with the claws and form of vultures or eagles. It was, indeed, the Sirens' more sinister features that persuaded Georg Weicker at the turn of the century that they were soul-birds in origin with vampirish proclivities. But although examples of soul-birds and kindred daemons are found in the art of Egypt and Anatolia, there is no evidence whatsoever that the soul was ever regarded as a bird by the Greeks, still less that the dead, whatever the true form and meaning of the Anthesterian injunction, were regarded as vampires, a folk-belief which the modern Hellenes adopted from the Slavs. Nevertheless the evidence collected in Weicker's *Grundwerk* helped to clarify the terms of a complex problem that

had not been seriously tackled before. Despite criticism, in particular by British scholars, Weicker's theory continued to hold the
field, and Zwicker in his article in Pauly-Wissowa contented himself with augmenting Weicker's material. Then, in 1932, Emil
Kunze advanced a new theory based on a study of a class of evidence largely discounted by Weicker. Many examples had come
to light of Sirens attached to bronze vessels manufactured during
the archaic period, and these Kunze maintained possessed a different history from the Sirens of the vases in as much as they had
been adopted direct, and without significant modification, from
oriental prototypes. They were, in his view, analogous in conception to the Griffins and Sphinxes which were the original
familiars of the Mistress of the Beasts, and represented the
visible embodiments of demonic forces—*sie verkörpern dämonische
Mächte.*

Wilamowitz too was intrigued by Sirens, and hazarded the view
that when associated with warriors they were intended to represent Keres, the individual dooms of the heroes concerned. But he
also quoted with approval Alcman's charming compliment to a
member of his chorus. 'The Muse did sing, the clear voiced
Siren.' Ernst Buschor's classic work *Die Musen des Jenseits*, which
appeared in 1944, untrammelled by a panoply of references and
notes, clearly owed much to Alcman's specious equation, and
the passage in Plutarch already quoted. For Buschor the Sirens
which appear in musical contexts are of primary importance,
and represent most nearly the daemon's essential nature. Just as
Apollo leads the chorus of the heavenly Muses, Zeus' daughters,
who inhabit the mountain tops and impart wisdom to men, so 'in
the clear ocean of space or the twilight of Hades dwell their
other-world counterparts, whose song may be heard only by the
departed'. Their function was both to solace the dead through the
medium of their unearthly music, and to act as emissaries between this world and the next, a rôle for which their ambiguous
appearance was admirably adapted. According to Buschor the
oriental Mischwesen excited the early artists' imagination, and
was employed by them to represent preying death-demons,
omens, deities' familiars, Homer's sea-monsters, whose appearance was not described in the *Odyssey*, as well as genuine Sirens.
Despite these abberrations the latter remained as always *Mächtige
Geister des Jenseits.*

Buschor's arguments are so persuasive that few have ventured to criticize his general thesis. Recently, however, Marót in an important work has, to use his favourite phrase, attacked Buschor and Kunze *ab ovo*. Marót considers, as had already been suggested, that Buschor went astray in attempting to deprive the Homeric ˉSirens of their essential priority. The Sirens of Homer were, according to him, the original pre-Sirens, which had nothing to do with the oriental Mischwesen. The legend about the Sirens' island probably, as Bérard had supposed, reached the Greeks through the Phoenicians, and was adopted by them as their own. During the archaic period an independent class of Sirens developed in the monuments which derived from oriental prototypes, and obscured the original legend. The label 'Siren' attached to the new monsters merely illustrates the familiar dictum that men tend to call new things by old names. Weicker and his school used the archaeological evidence to support their untenable theories, and were wrong, as Kunze saw, in supposing that the Greek Siren derived from Egypt. Kunze's own work was vitiated by his attempt to emphasize the importance of the Asiatic Mischwesen at the expense of the true Sirens. Marót derives Siren from the oriental root šir meaning fascination, and it is interesting to note that Simonides is reputed to have described Pisistratus as a Siren because he lured men to their doom. The original spell-binders of Phoenician legend were the prototypes of Homer's Sirens on the one hand, and of the tomb Sirens on the other. The rest developed alongside the Griffins and Sphinxes and other monsters, but were not in the true line of descent. Marót has in fact inverted Buschor's thesis without adding very much of his own.

The whole Siren problem seems past solution in the absence of literary evidence. The main difficulty, of course, is that the monuments, in the main, fail to support a consistent theory. It does, however, seem possible that growing concern with the fate of the individual after death helped the Siren to achieve its canonical form. In the *Odyssey* the monsters' offer of supernatural wisdom was open only to such as sailed to their magic isle. During the sixth century B.C. even the humblest were anxious to share such advantages as the underworld provided, and the Siren became a symbol of an otherwise near-inexpressible yearning for something akin to Paradise after death. Any attempt to rationalize the Greek artistic imagination during its era of final development is naturally doomed to failure. All we can do is to observe and study in the hope that some measure of understanding may one day dawn. Possibly there is less to understand from the strictly religious point of view than once appeared likely. Possibly again there is more.

The Sphinx has received only incidental mention. During the sixth century B.C. the oriental monster of the animal frieze became both humanized and individualized and eventually attached to the cult of Apollo. That she came to be regarded as his emissary seems clear from her dedication at Delphi. Her sinister connotation, like that of the Sirens, was never forgotten as is shown by her presence like them on tombs. Though she lacked the deeper implications of the *Musen des Jenseits* she belonged like them and the Satyrs and Sirens to the great No-man's land of folk-belief.

NOTES TO CHAPTER VIII

Page 137. Early Sirens. Cf. Kunze, 'Seirenen', *AM*, LVII, 1932; Payne, *Necrocorinthia*, p. 90, n. 3; Doro Levi, 'The Siren from Praisos', *AJA*, Supplement, 1945, pp. 280 ff.

Pedasians. Cf. Herodotus, I, 175. Here I acknowledge the kindness of Mr B. R. I. Sealey for supplying this reference.

Perachora. Cf. Buschor, *Die Musen des Jenseits*, fig. 8.

138. Boston Aryballos. Cf. Bulle, *Strena Helbigiana*, pp. 31 ff., fig. 178; Payne, op. cit., pl. 36.5; Möbius, *AM*, 1916, p. 211; Müller, *Die Antiken Odyssee-Illustrationen*, p. 31, n. 1.

Phallus. Cf. Weicker, *Der Seelenvogel*, pp. 43 ff.

Birds. Cf. Pollard, 'The Boston Siren Aryballos', *AJA*, LIII, 1949, pp. 347 ff.

Chthon. Cf. Jane Harrison, *Prolegomena to Greek Religion*, p. 200.

Design. Cf. Marót, *Die Anfänge der Griechischen Literatur*, p. 123.

Lekythos. Cf. Haspels, *Attic black-figured Lekythoi*, pp. 87, 158, n. 2, p. 217, pl. 29.3.

Naucratis. *BM* B103, 19.

139. Sirens' suicide. Cf. Lycophron, *Alex.*, 712 f., 1463; Weicker, op. cit., pp. 44 ff.

Stamnos. BM E440.

Harpy Tomb. BM *Cat. of Sculpture*, I, new ed., 1928.

Cyprus. Cf. Buschor, op. cit., fig. 26.

Laconian Cup. Cf. Lane, *BSA*, XXXIV, pp. 139, 158–9, and pl. 42B.

Karlsrühe. Cf. Weicker, op. cit., fig. 15.

Pinax. Cf. Weicker in *Roscher's Lexicon*, sv. *Seirenen*, fig. 3.

Theseus. Cf. Buschor, op. cit., fig. 16.

140. Procris. BM E477. Cf. Cook, *Zeus*, III, pl. 12 and p. 73, n. 5.

Exekias. Cf. Buschor, op. cit., p. 28.

Proto-Artemis. Cf. Langlotz, *Antike*, 8, 1932, pp. 175 ff.; Kunze, loc. cit., pp. 124 ff.

Mirrors. Cf. Buschor, op. cit., fig. 23; Papadimitriou, *The Times*, September 28, 1961; *Ergon*, 1962, pl. 28, p. 28.

Hera. Cf. Pausanias, IX, 34, 2; Buschor, op. cit., fig. 19.

Rome. Cf. Buschor, op. cit., p. 30.

Apollo. Cf. Buschor, op. cit., p. 53.

141. Music. Cf. Plato, *Repub.*, X, 617B; Plutarch, *Sympos.*, 745CD.

Dionysus. BM E14.

Tomb Sirens. Cf. Wilamowitz, *Glaube*, I, pp. 268 ff.

Pillar Sirens. Cf. Buschor, op. cit., figs. 45, 46, and pp. 39, 40 and 58.

142. Homeric Sirens. Cf. Pollard, 'Muses and Sirens', *CR*, LXVI, 1952, pp. 60 ff.; Marót, op. cit., pp. 134 ff. (Alcman, 14 (Loeb).)

143. Pisistratus. Cf. Bowra, *Greek Lyric Poets*[2], pp. 336 ff.

For possible connection between Siren and Sirius of K. Latte, *Festschrift der Göttinger Akademie*, 1951.

CHAPTER IX

THE STATE CULTS

—◦❧❦◦—

Only passing mention has been made of the innumerable cults and festivals which flourished outside Attica during the sixth century B.C. At Argos the position of Hera was analogous to that of Athena at Athens, and her temple at the Heraion was one of the oldest in mainland Greece. The massive foundations of the archaic temple may still be seen, as they were by Pausanias. It contained an ancient image carved out of the wood of the wild pear, and Pheidon, king of Argos, dedicated iron currency bars there in the seventh century B.C. Every year concourses of pious Argives set out for the distant hieron in much the same spirit, and perhaps with something of the same hopes as the Mystae wending their way to Eleusis. Of the details of the cult we know little, apart from what may be gleaned from the offerings revealed by the excavator's spade and Herodotus' description of the saintly Cleobis and Biton who drew their priestess mother to the temple in a waggon when the oxen failed to arrive, and were honoured, as has been seen, with statues at Delphi. There is a simplicity and sense of resignation about the tale which accords well with what is known about the archaic period. Indeed it is this feeling of powerlessness in the face of the resistless gods that probably accounts for the vast scale of the offerings of idols and figurines which is so characteristic of archaic sites in general.

There was also at Argos a contest for a shield in Hera's honour, which has been linked with Mycenaean religious practices. The ancient temple of Athena Oxyderkes, the Sharp-sighted, stood on the hill known as the Shield, which forms the lower acropolis. And Wolfish Apollo was also honoured at Argos as well as Artemis, Aphrodite, Demeter and other deities and heroes.

At Samos the cult of Hera had been long established and flourished under the tyrant Polycrates, who rebuilt her largest and finest temple. There was celebrated the strange festival of the Teneia when the goddess' statue was dragged down to the shore bound with strips of withe. All along the coasts of the Peloponnese Hera had her shrines, at Corinth, Sicyon and notably at Olympia. There her festival, the Heraea, included a girls' race which Drees believes originally formed part of a sacred marriage. But whether his thesis that the Olympic Games possessed a fertility origin be accepted or not there is no denying the grandeur of the seventh century temple and the goddess' obvious importance in archaic times. Even the barren Perachora isthmus could boast a remarkable sixth century temple dedicated to Hera. In such remote districts men continued to remain uninfluenced by wider religious movements, and honoured with increasing fervour the deities which they knew.

Sappho bears eloquent witness in poems which, as Sir Maurice Bowra noticed, amount virtually to cult-songs, to the power and influence of Aphrodite. Indeed she suggests that in her day, as always by true believers, the gods were regarded as real beings, who could visit and comfort their worshippers. Such a view would, of course, have considerable bearing on the circumstances surrounding the story of Phya, as well as the meeting between Pan and Philippides. Even the remote summit of Mount Cotilius in Arcadia could boast a shrine of Aphrodite, but in Corinth she was worshipped with such oriental rites as religious prostitution, which reflect on her ultimate origin.

Apollo too was naturally honoured at Corinth on the coast fronting Delphi.

In Laconia Apollo absorbed the heroic cults of Hyacinthus and Carnos, like that of Ptous in Boeotia, and so increased their fame. The Carnea and Hyacinthea became notable festivals instead of mere local feasts. Athena too possessed a temple hung with shields of bronze in the city of her rivals, but Orthia was the goddess whom the Spartan aristocracy revered with dancing, music and processions on horseback as at the Hyacinthea. Whether the rites included flagellation of the ephebes during the archaic period has been hotly debated, but the evidence is late and therefore suspect for pre-Roman times.

Flagellation was practised at Delos too, though the tradition is confused. Whether the altar of Apollo, his worshippers or both were beaten remains obscure. The story that Polycrates sought guidance from Delphi as to whether he should rename a ceremony 'Pythia' or 'Delia' supports the evidence of the Homeric Hymn that the pan-Ionian festival rivalled that of the oracle in archaic Greece. In point of fact Delos possessed an oracle itself, at least in later times. Certainly Athens, as the leading Ionian power, had always been anxious to gain control of the festival, and Pisistratus, with an eye on the Cyclades, purified Delos about 543 B.C. He did so by opening the tombs within sight of the sanctuary and removing the dead to other parts of the isle. Purifications were, of course, much in vogue during the sixth century, but this was katharsis on the grand scale. The overt reason for the tyrant's action was political, but it was also well calculated to recommend both himself and the city which he represented to the special protection of the god.

Second only in importance to the cult of Apollo was that of the Titaness who had given him birth. During the sixth century B.C. a temple was built in Delos to shelter the ancient wooden image which was worshipped in her name. Its size suggests that the goddess was revered before her daughter Artemis. Strangely enough Hera, Leto's relentless rival, was honoured with a shrine of more venerable antiquity contemporaneous with the Artemisium. But then she had long acquired both here and in Samos the kind of oriental affinities which Artemis inherited at Ephesus, and Magnesia, where Anacreon honoured her in a famous poem.

Poseidon's tufa temple on stormy cape Sunium was certain to awaken the piety of sailors. Indeed all his chief shrines, including those at the Isthmus and Paestum, were naturally built beside the sea. Athena too was frequently worshipped alongside her rival in archaic times as her temples at Sunium, Sigeum and Lindos show. But the latter cult included fireless ritual, a chthonian feature, which in origin had nothing to do with Athena at all. Helios again was only worshipped in Rhodes, and such cults as that of Ataburion Zeus were curiously un-Greek.

Thebes was rich in ancient cults as Pausanias bears witness, and both Pindar and Herodotus bear witness to the golden tripods kept there, engraved with antique characters. Most famous was that of the Ismenian Apollo with its curious annual custom of electing a boy priest. The altar of the Spodian Apollo has already been mentioned, and naturally there were cults of Dionysus. Again the presence of wooden images of Heracles, and of Aphro-

dite Urania and Pandemos, suggest that their worship had been
long established.

Zeus and Hera were honoured at the festival of the Daedala,
whose ritual includes seemingly primitive features. Boiled flesh
was put out in a wood near Alalcomenae, and a watch kept to discover which crow first pounced on it. The tree to which it flew
was then marked down, and felled to make a *daidalon*, i.e. a
wooden image. The image was subsequently decked and laid
in a waggon with a bridesmaid for company, and driven from the
river Asopus to the summit of mount Cithaeron, where a cow
and a bull were sacrificed to Hera and Zeus respectively. Every
sixtieth year—perhaps a solar interval—the festival was celebrated with greater magnificence by all the Boeotians, who drew
lots for the *daidala*, which had been meantime preserved.

Also at Alalcomenae was an ancient temple of Athena. According to Strabo the goddess was said to have been born there, and
both the city and its inhabitants were regarded as inviolable. Indeed it became a centre for refugees after the expedition of the
Epigoni, the sons of the legendary Seven heroes who had originally attacked Thebes. Nothing, however, is recorded of the ritual
practised there.

Athena Onca is mentioned by Aeschylus. The goddess' altar
and image stood in the open, and her association with the snake
which Cadmus killed suggest that she was originally an independent deity whose worship was connected with the fertility of
the earth. Her cult had been absorbed in fact like that of Alea at
Tegea in Arcadia, though others such as that of Aphaia in Aegina
continued to remain distinct.

More important was the cult of Itonian Athena at Coronea, the
rallying place of the Boeotian League. Her fame was known to
Alcaeus, who addresses her as Polemadoke—Sustainer of War—
though Bacchylides refers to Itonia as a patroness of poetry.

All that we know of the ritual practised there was that it was
a woman's duty to put fire on the altar of Iodama, an unfortunate
former priestess who was said to have been transformed into stone
by sight of the Gorgon's head, and proclaim that she was still
alive and demanding fire.

Cults of Hermes are comparatively speaking rare. But the god
was honoured at Thebes under the rustic title of *Kriophoros*—
Ram-bearer—a familiar motif in archaic art, while Eros was

worshipped at Thespiae near Helicon as well as Heracles and the Muses.

Pindar pays a charming tribute to the rustic Charites whose worship was especially associated with Orchomenus, while the shrine of Apollo Ptous, at whose oracle Mys the Carian once received a response in his own tongue, was honoured with a dedication from the Pisistratid Hipparchus.

Sherds dating from the Geometric period, as well as a considerable number dating from the sixth century B.C., prove that the Cabeirion near Thebes was in use long before the time of the Athenian Methapus who was credited by Pausanias with having instituted the mysteries there. Whether Guthrie is right in supposing Dionysiac or Orphic influence is an open question, though there was apparently some contamination with Demeter at the shrine of the Cabeiroi at Anthedon. The history of the Great Gods at Samothrace is equally obscure, though the old temple dates from the sixth century B.C. Hermes too was worshipped there and also at Lemnos, the ancient Pelasgian centre of the worship of Hephaestus.

It is hard to pronounce with any certainty on the age of the Arcadian cults. Certainly Artemis, Hermes, Pan and Zeus had been worshipped there from time immemorial in one form or another. But Pausanias is not evidence for the sixth century B.C. and though ancient votive offerings were found on the site of the temple of the Mistress at Lycosura, we have no means of gauging the age of the cults of Pan or Apollo on Mount Lycaeus, although that of Zeus dates from the seventh century B. C. a like objection applies to the worship of Hermes on Mount Cyllene and the Acacesian Hill, though he is associated with the mountain in the Homeric Hymn, and of Artemis Opis in Lacedaemon and at Troezen.

In the far north Dodona's fame was still sufficient to attract Croesus, if we can believe Herodotus, though it inevitably ranked second to Delphi. Indeed the influence of Delphi on what was generally regarded as the oldest oracle in Greece is suggested by the substitution of three prophetesses in place of the Selloi, probably during the sixth century B.C., as well as the institution of a lot oracle. Queries were scratched on lead plates and placed in a jar, from which they were drawn by a priestess and answered without being unfolded.

In addition to the great athletic festivals local contests were held at many centres. The Brazen Contest at Argos has already been mentioned. Games were also held at Thebes in honour of Iolaus, Heracles' companion, at Lebadeia, on Helicon in honour of Eros, at Pellene in Achaea in honour of Hermes, on Mount Lycaeus in Arcadia in honour of Zeus, and at Megara. Probably most were instituted in imitation of the more famous festivals, and all were doubtless influenced by them. Pindar, at any rate, was familiar with most of them, and it is reasonable to place their foundation or revival some time after the Pythian during the sixth century B.C.

Attica herself supported innumerable cults during the archaic period, as we have already had occasion to observe. Some like that of Nemesis at Rhamnous and the mysteries of Earth at Phlya which, according to the Christian Hippolytus, antedated those at Eleusis, all but rivalled those of Athens, and maintained their independence despite their proximity to the capital.

To have attempted a detailed survey of all the cults known or surmised to have existed in Greece during the sixth century B.C. could have only ended in tedium and defeated the purpose of this book. The whole point of taking a synoptic view is to hope that it may reveal some trends. If anything has emerged from the foregoing survey it is the new-found importance of the ordinary individual during a century when, to quote Detienne, 'no demand was manifested for an objective knowledge of the past'. In an era of credulity prophets flourish, while the protests of reason only begin to be heard. In Asia the sixth century produced Gautama and Lao-Tsu as well as Deutero-Isaiah. In Greece it saw the appearance of shamans like Epimenides, as well as of revolutionary thinkers like Pythagoras and the leaders of the Orphic movement. But of equal importance and complementary to them were the pilgrims visiting Delphi or flocking to Eleusis. Politically too it was an age of effervescence when the urgent attempts of tyrants to achieve greatness gave a brilliant new impetus to established religion. It is difficult to think of the sixth century B.C. apart from such men as Pisistratus and Polycrates, Alyattes and Croesus, whose influence was as all-pervading in the spiritual as in the political sphere. So much the penumbral spotlight has revealed. Much still is dark. The publication of the spectacular finds made at Brauron, Thebes and elsewhere in Greece and Anatolia will doubtless serve to illuminate many obscure corners. At the same time the historian of religion cannot but be painfully aware of Kierkegaard's dictum that no systemization is valid, whether it be of philosophy or men's beliefs, because it is seen from the outside. Like the Delphic oracle he can only hope to hint at the truth.

NOTES TO CHAPTER IX

Page 146. Temple of Hera. Cf. Pausanias, II, 17, 7; Amandry, *Hesp.*, 1952.

Cleobis and Biton. Cf. Herodotus, I, 31; Pausanias, II, 20, 2; Cicero, *Tusc.*, I, 47.

Offerings. Cf. Payne, *Necrocorinthia*, p. 185.

Shield. Cf. Pindar, *Ol.* VII, 83, and scholium, XIII, 107; Nem., X, 22; Arnold, *AJA*, 41, pp. 43 ff.

Athena. Cf. Volgraff, *Mnemosyne*, LVI, p. 319.

Apollo. Cf. Sophocles, *Electra*, 6 f.

Samos. Cf. Dinsmoor, *Ancient Architecture*, pp. 135 ff.

147. Teneia. Cf. Athenaeus, XV, 672DE.

Olympia. Cf. Drees, *Der Ursprung der Olympischen Spiele;* Mehl, *Mütterrechtliche Reste in der Olympischen Festordnung.*

Perachora. Cf. Payne, *Perachora*, I, pp. 78 ff.

Aphrodite. Cf. Pindar, *fgm.* 87; Bowra, *Greek Lyric Poetry*[2], pp. 196 ff.; Pollard, *G&R*, XXII, 67, 1954, pl. CXXXIV, fig. 4.

Apollo. Cf. Weinberg, *Hesperia* VIII, pp. 191 ff.

Hyacinthus, Carnos. Cf. Pausanias, III, 13, 3; 19, 3; Mellink, *Hyakinthos;* Chrimes, *Ancient Sparta*, p. 270.

Ptous. Cf. Herbillon, *Les Trépieds du Ptoin.*

Athena. Cf. Thucydides, I, 134.

Orthia. Cf. Dawkins, *The Sanctuary of Artemis Orthia at Sparta.*

Flagellation. Cf. Chrimes, op. cit., 260 ff.; Gallet de Santerre, *Délos Primitive et Archaique*, pp. 184–6.

148. Pisistratus. Cf. Herodotus I, 64; Thucydides, III, 104.

Leto. Cf. Gallet de Santerre, op. cit., pp. 257–8.

Artemis. Cf. Bowra, op. cit., pp. 273 ff.

Isthmus. Cf. Broneer, *Hesperia*, 1958, pp. 10–15; 1962, pp. 1 ff.

Sigeum. Cf. Herodotus, V, 95.

Lindos. Cf. Pindar, *Ol.* VII, 47 ff., and Farnell, ad loc.

Thebes. Cf. Pindar, *Pyth.*, X, 8 f.; Herodotus, V, 59; Pausanias, IX, 16 f.

149. Daedala. Cf. Pausanias, IX, 3, 3.

    Alalcomenae. Cf. Pausanias, IX, 33, 5; Strabo, IX, 413.

    Onca. Cf. *Septem*, 164, 487, 501; Farnell, *CGS*, I, p. 300.

    Alea. Cf. Pausanias, VIII, 45, 3; Nilsson, *Geschichte*[2], I, p. 552.

    Itonian Athena. Cf. Alcaeus *fgm*. 6 (Loeb); Bacchylides, *fgm*. 23; Pausanias, IX, 34.

    Hermes. Cf. Pausanias, IX, 22, and Frazer, ad loc.

150. Thespiae. Cf. Pausanias, IX, 27.

    Charites. Cf. Pindar, *Ol.* XIV.

    Cabeirion. Cf. Pausanias, IV, 1, 5; Guthrie, *Orpheus*, pp. 123 ff.; Hemberg, *Die Kabiren*, pp. 186; Lehmann, *Samothrace*.

    Anthedon. Cf. Pausanias, IX, 22, 5; Hemberg, op. cit., pp. 53, 66 ff., 137.

    Hermes. Cf. Herodotus, II, 51.

    Lemnos. Cf. Aeschylus, *Agamemnon*, 282.

    Lycosura. Cf. Pausanias, VIII, 37.

    Lycaeus. The cult of Zeus was known to Alcam (fgms. 4, 6, 7, 9, 10, Diehl) and bronze statuettes found on the mountain date from the seventh century B. C. Cf. Cook, *Zeus* I, p. 84. For wolf cults cf. Eckels, *Greek Wolflore*, 1937. For archaic temple of Apollo at Bassae of *Ergon*, 1960, 106f.

    Hermes. *Homeric Hymn to Hermes*, 218; Pausanias, VIII, 17; 36, 6.

    Opis. Cf. Farnell, *CGS*, II, pp. 486 ff.

    Dodona. Cf. Herodotus, I, 46; II, 52; Parke, *Proc. Class. Assoc.*, 1963.

151. Minor festivals. Cf. Farnell ad *Ol.* VII, 83 f.

    Rhamnous. Cf. Pausanias, I, 33, 2.

    Phlya. Cf. Pausanias, I, 31, 4.

    The precise status of the cult of Hestia, goddess of the hearth, is uncertain in archaic times. She was worshipped in the council chambers (Pind. Nem XI) and in association with Apollo at Delphi (Hom. Hymn XXIV and Plut. Num. 9). For her association with Hermes of Hom. Hymn XXIX and J. P. Vernant, *Mythe et Pensée chez les Grecs*, 1965, ch. 3.

SELECT BIBLIOGRAPHY

—o❧❦o—

Amandry, P., *La Mantique Apollinienne à Delphes*, 1950.

Bouché-Leclercq, A., *Histoire de la Divination dans l'Antiquité*, 1879–82.

Bowra, Sir C. M., *Greek Lyric Poets*[2], 1961.
'A fragment of the Arimaspeia', *CQ*, 1956, pp. 1 ff.

Brommer, F., *Satyroi*, 1937; *Satyrspiele*, 1959.

Burn, A. R., *The Lyric Age of Greece*, 1960.

Buschor, E., *Die Musen des Jenseits*, 1944.

Caskey, J. L., *Investigations in Keos*, 1963, *Hesperia*, 1964.

Chittenden, J., 'The Master of Animals', *Hesperia*, xv, 1947, pp. 89 ff.
'Diaktoros Argeiphontes', *AJA*, 1948, pp. 24 ff.

Chrimes, K. M. T., *Ancient Sparta*, 1949.

Cook, A. B., *Zeus*, 1914–40.

Corbett, P. E., 'The Burgos and Blacas Tombs', *JHS*, lxxx, 1960, pp. 52 ff.

Cornford, F. M., *Mysticism and Science in the Pythagorean Tradition*, *CQ*, xvi, 1922, pp. 137 ff.; xvii, 1923, pp. 1 ff.

Davison, J. A., 'Notes on the Panathenaea', *JHS*, lxxviii, 1958, pp. 23 ff.

Defradas, V., *Les Thèmes de la Propagande Delphique*, 1954.

· Delcourt, M., *L'Oracle de Delphes*, 1955.
Pyrrhos et Pyrrha, 1965.

Deubner, L., *Attische Feste*, 1932.

Dickins, Guy, *Catalogue of the Acropolis Museum*, 1912.

Diels, H., and Kranz, W., *Die Fragmente der Vorsokratikor*[7], 1954.

Dinsmoor, W. B., 'The Hekatompedon on the Athenian Acropolis', *AJA*, li, 1947.
Architecture of Ancient Greece, 1950.

Dittenberger, W. K. F., *Sylloge*[4], 1960.
Orientis Graecae Inscriptiones Selectae, 1960.

Dodds, E. R., *The Greeks and the Irrational*, 1951.
Euripides Bacchae[2], 1960.

D'Ooge, M. L., *The Acropolis of Athens*, 1908.

Drees, L., *Der Ursprung der Olympischen Spiele*, Stuttgart, 1962.

Dunbabin, T. J., *Greece and her Eastern Neighbours*, 1957.

Edelstein, E. and L., *Asclepius*, 1945.

Elderkin, G. W., *Studies in Early Athenian Cult, III*, in *Classical Studies presented to Edward Capps*, 1936.

Farnell, L. R., *Cults of the Greek States*, 1896–1909.

Greek Hero Cults and Ideas of Immortality, 1921.

Ferguson, W. S., *The Salaminioi of Heptaphylai and Sounion*, Hesperia, 7, No. 1, 1938, pp. 1 ff.

The Attic Orgeones HThR, 1944, pp. 61 ff.

Fontenrose, J., *Python. A Study of Delphic Myth and its Origins*, 1959.

The Cult and Myth of Pyrrhos at Delphi, 1961.

Forrest, W. G., *The First Sacred War, BCH*, 80, 1956.

Colonization and the Rise of Delphi, Historia, 1957, pp. 160 ff.

Frazer, Sir James, *Pausanias*, 1898.

The Golden Bough[3], 1932–8.

Gallet de Santerre, H., *Délos primitive et archaïque*, 1958.

Gardner, E., *A Handbook of Greek Sculpture*, 1915.

Guillon, A. P., *Les Trépieds du Ptoion*, 1943.

Guthrie, W. K. C., *Orpheus and Greek Religion*,[2] 1952.

The Greeks and their Gods, 1950.

Harrison, J. E., *Prolegomena to the Study of Greek Religion*[3], 1922.

Hege, W., *Griechische Tempel*, 1951.

Hemberg, B., *Die Kabiren*, 1950.

Herington, C. J., *Athena Parthenos and Athena Polias*, 1955.

Parthenos and Parthenon. G&R Supp. 1963.

Hignett, C., *A History of the Athenian Constitution*[2], (1952).

Hill, I. T., *The Ancient City of Athens*, 1953.

Holland, L. B., *The Mantic Mechanism at Delphi, AJA*, xxxvii, 1933, pp. 201 ff.

Hooker, G. T. W., *The Topography of the Frogs, JHS* lxxx, 1960, pp. 112 ff.

Jeffery, L. H., *The Local Scripts of Archaic Greece*, 1961.

Judeich, W., *Topographie von Athen*[2], 1931.

Kerenyi, C., *Asklepios, Archetypal Image of the Physician's Existence*, 1960.

Kern, O., *Orphicorum Fragmenta*, 1922.

Kirk, G. S., and Raven, J. E., *The Presocratic Philosophers*, 1957.

Klees, H., *Die Eigenart des griechischen Glaubens an Orakel und Seher*, 1965.

SELECT BIBLIOGRAPHY

Koller, H., *Dithyrambos und Tragödie, Glotta*, 1962, pp. 183 ff.

Kunze, E., *Seirenen, AM*, LVII, 1932.

Latte, K., *The Coming of the Pythia. HThR*, XXXIII, 1940.

Die Sirenen, Festschrift der Göttinger Akademie, 1951.

Römische Religionsgeschichte, 1960.

Lawson, J. C., *Modern Greek Folklore and Ancient Greek Religions*, 1910.

Leaf, W., *Strabo on the Troad*, 1923.

Levi, Doro. *Gleanings from Crete, AJA*, XLIX, 1945, No. 3, pp. 27off.

Linforth, I. M., *The Arts of Orpheus*, 1941.

Marót, K., *Die Anfänge der griechischen Literatur*, 1960.

Mason, P. G., *Kassandra, JHS*, LXXIX, 1959.

Mellink, J., *Hyakinthos*, 1943.

Möbius, H., *Form und Bedeutung der Sitzende Gestalt, AM*, LXXII, 1916.

Morrison, J. S., *Pythagoras of Samos, CQ*, 1956, pp. 135 ff.

Mylonas, G. E., *The Hymn to Demeter and her Sanctuary at Eleusis*, 1942.

Eleusis and the Eleusinian Mysteries, 1961.

Nilsson, M. P., *Early Orphism and Kindred Religious Movements, HThR*, XXVIII, 1935, pp. 181 ff.

Geschichte der Griechischen Religion[2], 1955.

Das Delphische Orakel in der neusten Literatur, Historia, 7, 1958.

Nock, A. D., *The Cult of Heroes HThR*, 1944, pp. 141 ff.

Orlandos, A., *La fontaine découverte à Delphes, BCH*, LXXXIV, 1960, pp. 148 ff.

Otto, W., *Dionysos*, 1933.

Page, Denys, *Sappho and Alcaeus*, 1955.

Palmer, L. R., *The Interpretation of Mycenaean Greek Texts*, 1963.

Papadimitriou, J., *Uncovering a Greek Legend, The Times*, Sept. 28, 1961.

Parke, H. W., and Wormell, D. E. W., *A History of the Delphic Oracle*, 1956.

Payne, Humfry, *Necrocorinthia*, 1931.

Perachora I, 1940.

Payne, H., and Young, *Archaic Marble Sculpture from the Acropolis*[2] (1936).

Pfeiffer, R., *The Image of the Delian Apollo and Apolline Ethics. Journal of the Warburg and Courtauld Institute*, XV, 1952.

Pickard-Cambridge, A. W., *Dithyramb Tragedy and Comedy*[2], 1962.

The Theatre of Dionysus at Athens, 1946.

The Dramatic Festivals of Athens, 1953.

Plommer, W. H., *The Archaic Acropolis, AJA*, LXXX, 1960, pp. 127 ff.

Pollard, J. R. T., *The Lammergeyer. Comparative descriptions in Aristotle and Pliny, G&R*, 1947, pp. 23 ff.

Birds in Aeschylus, G&R, 1948, pp. 116 ff.

The Birds of Aristophanes—a source book for old beliefs. *AJP*, 1948, pp. 353 ff.

The Boston Siren Aryballos, AJA, 1949, pp. 357 ff.

Muses and Sirens, CR, LXVI, 1952, pp. 60 ff.

Delphica, BSA, 55, 1960, pp. 195 ff.

Helen of Troy, 1965.

Poulsen, F., *Delphi*, 1920.

Raubitschek, A. E., *Dedications from the Athenian Akropolis*, 1949.

Ridgeway, Sir William, *The Origin of Tragedy*, 1910.

Roberts, E. S., *An Introduction to Greek Epigraphy*, 1887.

Rohde, E., *Psyche*[8], Hillis, 1925.

Rose, H. J., *A Handbook of Greek Mythology*[6], 1958.

Ancient Greek Religion, 1946.

The Ancient Grief in Greek Poetry and Life. Essays presented to Gilbert Murray on his seventieth birthday, 1936, pp. 79 ff.

Tod, M. N., *A Selection of Greek Historical Inscriptions*[2], 1946.

Travlos, J., *Poleodomike exelixis ton Athenon*, 1960.

Usener, H., *Götternamen*[3], 1948.

Vanderpool, E., *The Route of Pausanias in the Athenian Agora, Hesperia* 18, 1949, pp. 128 ff.

Newsletter from Greece, AJA, 63, 1959, pp. 1 ff.

Vernant, J. P., *Mythe et Pensée chez les Grecs*, 1965.

Wade-Gery, H. T., *Kynaithos in Greek Poetry and Life*, 1936, pp. 56 ff.

Wagenvoort, H., *Roman Dynamism*, 1947.

Walcot, P., *Text of Hesiod's Theogony and the Hittite epic of the Kumarbi, CQ*, 1956, VI, pp. 198 ff.

Webster, T. B. L., *From Mycenae to Homer*.

Greek Art and Literature, 700–530 B.C., 1959.

Wilamowitz-Moellendorf, U. von, *Der Glaube der Hellenen*, 1932.

Wycherley, R. E., *Athenian Agora III, Testimonia*, 1957.

Two Athenian Shrines, AJA, 1959, pp. 67 ff.

Neleion, BSA, LV, 1960, pp. 61 ff.

The Pythion at Athens, AJA, 1963, pp. 75 ff; *The Olympieion at Athens, Greek, Roman* and *Byzantine Studies*, 1964.

INDEX

INDEX

INDEX

INDEX

INDEX

163

INDEX